BASEBALL NOW!

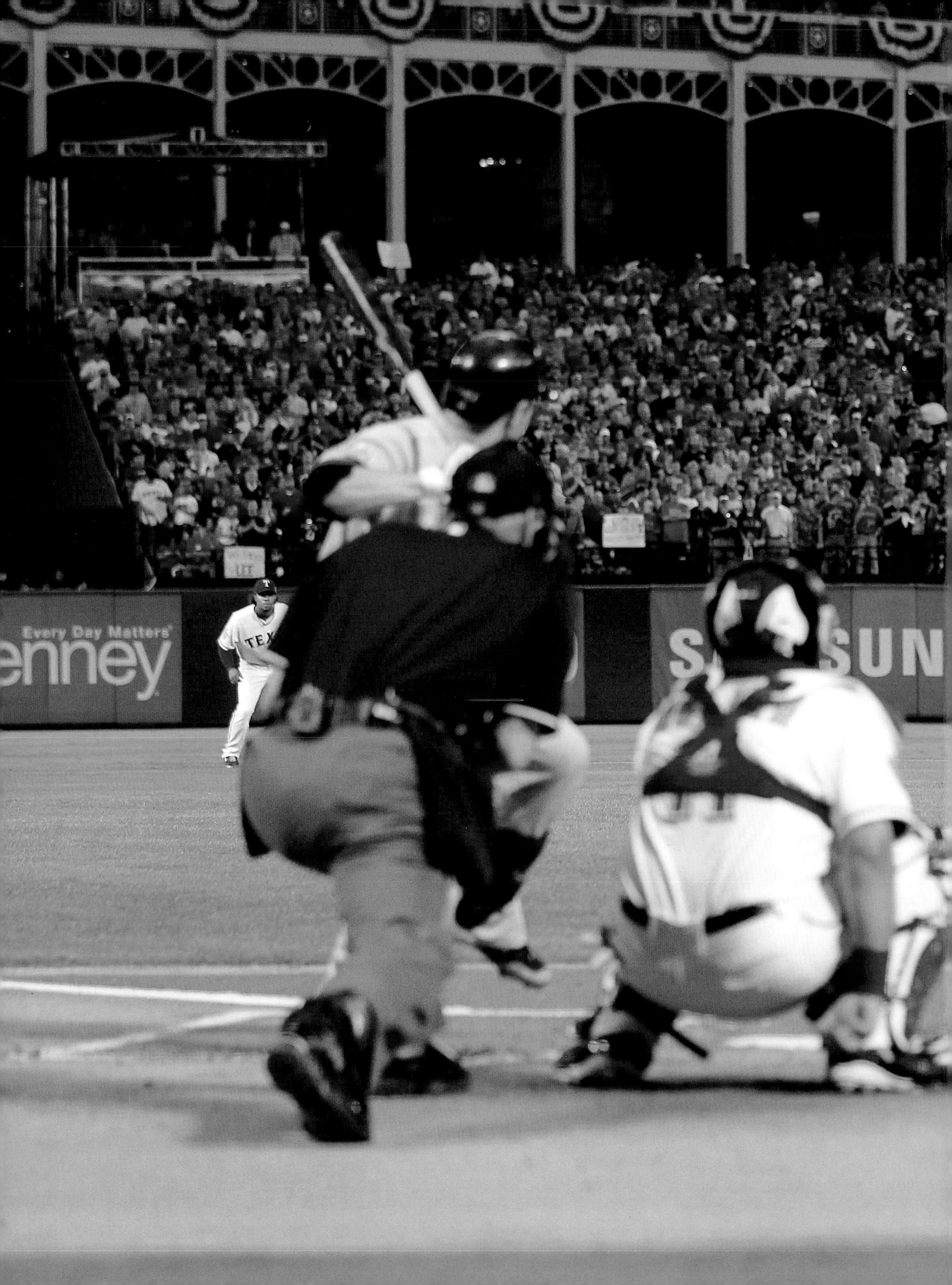
Every Day Matters
enney
TEX

BASEBALL NOW!

SECOND EDITION

DAN BORTOLOTTI

FIREFLY BOOKS

A FIREFLY BOOK

Published by Firefly Books Ltd. 2011

First printing

Publisher Cataloging-in-Publication Data (U.S.)

Bortolotti, Dan.
    Baseball now! / Dan Bortolotti. 2nd ed.
[160] p. : photos. ; cm.
Includes index.
Summary: Features player profiles as well as up-to-date coverage of the 2010 regular season, playoffs and World Series.

ISBN-13: 978-1-55407-826-4
ISBN-10: 1-55407-826-1

    1. Baseball players – Biography. 2. Baseball. I. Title.
796.357092/2 dc22   GV865.A1B67 2011

Library and Archives Canada Cataloguing in Publication

Bortolotti, Dan
        Baseball now! / Dan Bortolotti. -- 2nd ed.

ISBN-13: 978-1-55407-826-4
ISBN-10: 1-55407-826-1

    1. Baseball players--Biography. 2. Baseball. I. Title.
GV865.A1B67 2011   796.357092'2   C2010-907686-9

Published in the United States by
Firefly Books (U.S.) Inc.
P.O. Box 1338, Ellicott Station
Buffalo, New York 14205

Published in Canada by
Firefly Books Ltd.
66 Leek Crescent
Richmond Hill, Ontario L4B 1H1

Cover and interior design: Luna Design

Printed in Canada

The publisher gratefully acknowledges the financial support for our publishing program by the Government of Canada through the Canada Book Fund as administered by the Department of Canadian Heritage.

For my dad, who first brought me to the ballpark, and for Jaimie and Erick, who brought me back

Photo Credits

Reuters Pictures

Scott Audette 19, 52, 67, 128; Keith Bedford 75; Mike Blake 5 bottom horizontal, 9, 21, 27, 33, 35, 129, 132, 133, 142, 158 top; Mark Blinch 5 top horizontal, 17; Anthony Bolante 5 top right, 34, 103, 112, 113; Mike Cassese 25, 37, 54, 73; Tami Chappell 59, 84, 114, 115, 136; Richard Clement 76; Jason Cohn 156 right; Sarah Conard 58, 86, 87, 107, 145; Rebecca Cook 30, 31, 41, 43, 65, 134, 155 left; Hans Deryk 60, 119, 148; Larry Downing 157 right; Jonathan Ernst 77, 92, 93; Allen Fredrickson 45; Robert Galbraith 88, 89, 95, 141, 143, 150, 151, 156 left, 157 left; Alex Gallardo 15, 26, 154 middle; Joe Giza 53, 57, 63, 147; Jeff Haynes 44, 153; Lisa Hornak 146; Adam Hunger 56, 96, 99, 122; Lucas Jackson 5 top left, 130; Dave Kaup 80, 81, 108, 109; Bill Kostroun 49; Mark Leffingwell 24, 68; Eric Miller 10, 16, 42, 51, 55, 79, 82, 83, 91, 94, 100, 101, 105; Danny Moloshok 14, 97, 138, 139, 158 middle; Peter Newcomb 106, 118; Lucy Nicholson 12, 20, 69; Frank Polich 32; POOL New 110, 116, 121, 124, 127; Jessica Rinaldi 149; Mike Segar 22, 50, 64; Tim Shaffer 5 bottom right, 47, 70, 71, 111; Tim Sharp 23, 36; Brian Snyder 123, 125, 126, 154 right; John Sommers II 13, 72, 144; Mike Stone 120, 154 left; Ray Stubblebine 18, 46, 48, 61, 62, 66, 74, 85, 131, 135, 137, 156 middle, 158 bottom; Fred Thornhill 5 bottom left, 11; Winslow Townson 98, 155 middle; Kimberley White 104; Rick Wilking 117

Getty Images

Hannah Foslien/Stringer 155 right; Leon Halip 39; Mitchell Layton 38, 157 middle; Bob Levey/Stringer 28, 29; Doug Pensinger 2–3; Christian Petersen 6–7, 160

Cover: Left: **Reuters Pictures** – Ray Stubblebine; Right: **Getty Images** - Otto Greule Jr.

Back Cover: Reuters Pictures – Eric Miller

contents

Most days I can't remember what I had for breakfast, but I rarely forget what I see on the baseball diamond. As a kid, one of my favorite books retold the stories of the sport's greatest moments from long before my time — like Ted Williams surpassing .400 on the last day of the 1941 season, and Willie Mays' over-the-shoulder catch in the 1954 World Series. I could recite the details of all of them. At the time, I never imagined I'd one day be witness to one of those magical moments myself. But there I was in the right-field bleachers at Toronto's SkyDome on October 23, 1993, when Joe Carter blasted a three-run walk-off homer to give the Blue Jays their second straight World Series title. I don't imagine I'll ever forget that one.

No other sport offers so many opportunities for great moments like these. Baseball's 162-game schedule means that almost every day, from April through October, includes countless one-on-one confrontations between pitcher and batter. Staring at each other across 60 feet, 6 inches, these players can go from hero to goat in a split-second — the time it takes for a fastball to whiz past a hitter, or a hanging curveball to be delivered to the upper deck. As the cliché goes, baseball is a game of inches, where the finest line separates a two-out walk from an inning-ending strikeout, a dramatic stolen base from a rally-killing out, and a foul ball from a game-winning home run. Baseball is also one of the few team sports with no clock — so it truly ain't over until it's over.

More than 73 million fans walked through MLB turnstiles in 2010. A decade ago, that lofty attendance figure would have been hard to predict. Indeed, from the mid-1990s until well into the new millennium, baseball was in crisis. The 1994 players' strike wiped out the postseason for the first time in history and fans rebelled: attendance the previous year had spiked at 70.2 million, but in 1995 it plummeted by 30 percent. I was one of the disillusioned. A year after Joe Carter gave me my fondest baseball memory, I lost interest in the game I had loved for so many years.

The power-hitting heroics of Mark McGwire and Sammy Sosa awakened fans in 1998, but attendance declined again every season from 2000 to 2003, as it became clear that steroids were a main reason for the rash of home runs. The lowest point may have come in the second half of the 2002 campaign, when yet another players' strike seemed imminent. But since those dark days, baseball is enjoying a renaissance. There are a few reasons for this. The wild card system has helped more small market teams compete for postseason berths — clubs in New York, Boston and Los Angeles continue to be successful, but they're being challenged by teams in Tampa, St. Louis, Colorado and Minnesota.

America's national pastime is also becoming increasingly international. The emergence of Asian-born stars, especially, is enriching the game the way European players revolutionized the National Hockey League. Baseball has also made strides toward preventing the use of banned substances.

Finally, there are the ballparks. The era of cavernous domes and plastic grass has all but come to an end. Only two of MLB's 30 stadiums still have artificial turf, and Tampa's Tropicana Field is the only one with a permanently closed roof. In the last decade, long-suffering fans in cities like Seattle, Minnesota, Houston, Cincinnati, Philadelphia and St. Louis have finally been able to watch baseball as it was meant to be played — in the sunshine, on real grass.

I've seen my own enthusiasm for the sport return, too. In recent years I've taken my family to games in San Diego, Pittsburgh, Detroit, New York and Boston, and watched my kids develop the same passion for baseball that I had at their age.

Of course, what brings fans of all ages to the ballparks is the players. This second edition of *Baseball Now!* celebrates the best pitchers and hitters in the game today: the athletes who have given us a generation of great moments, and who have helped shape the golden era of the grand old game.

INTRODUCTION

JOSE BAUTISTA - Toronto Blue Jays

JASON BAY - New York Mets

RYAN BRAUN - Milwaukee Brewers

SHIN-SOO CHOO - Cleveland Indians

CARL CRAWFORD - Boston Red Sox

ANDRE ETHIER - Los Angeles Dodgers

JOSH HAMILTON - Texas Rangers

MATT HOLLIDAY - St. Louis Cardinals

TORII HUNTER - Los Angeles Angels of Anaheim

CARLOS LEE - Houston Astros

MAGGLIO ORDONEZ - Detroit Tigers

ALFONSO SORIANO - Chicago Cubs

ICHIRO SUZUKI - Seattle Mariners

VERNON WELLS - Los Angeles Angels of Anaheim

CHRIS YOUNG - Arizona Diamondbacks

Outstanding
OUTFIELDERS

jose BAUTISTA

TORONTO BLUE JAYS ◆ AL East

Only 26 players in MLB history have clubbed 50 home runs in a season, and none was more of a surprise than Jose Bautista. The Blue Jays' right fielder had never hit more than 16 homers in his previous four campaigns, so his power display in 2010 was as unexpected as it was remarkable.

Born in Santo Domingo, Dominican Republic, Bautista was an excellent student, and when he was 18 he won a scholarship to a Florida college. Two years later, the Pittsburgh Pirates chose him in the 20th round of the 2000 draft. Bautista played three seasons in the Bucs' minor league system, but in 2003 the team left him off their 40-man roster, which made him eligible for the Rule 5 draft that December. The Baltimore Orioles grabbed him with the idea of using him as a backup infielder.

Thanks to a whirlwind series of deals in 2004, Bautista became the only player to spend time on five different MLB rosters in one season. After the Orioles placed him on waivers, he was passed around like a hot potato by the Devil Rays, Royals and Mets before ending up back in Pittsburgh. Bautista finally enjoyed regular playing time in 2006, when he hit 16 home runs. He added 15 more the following year, but struggled to keep his average above .250, and by August 2008 even the last-place Pirates didn't want Bautista in the lineup. They demoted him to Triple-A and were happy to unload him when the Blue Jays showed interest.

The Jays played Bautista at third base and in the outfield in 2009, but he didn't become a regular until

September. He smacked his fourth home run of the season on September 7, homered again three days later, and picked up another pair at Yankee Stadium. Then he ended the season with an explosion of five jacks in his last six games, foreshadowing what was to come in 2010.

When Bautista hit .439 with five home runs in spring training, he easily got the nod as the Jays' right fielder and leadoff man on Opening Day. He slumped in the early going and was batting .206 in early May, but then launched 12 long balls in his next 83 at-bats. Manager Cito Gaston dropped Bautista to the number-three spot in the order, and by the break the slugger was leading the majors with 24 homers and was selected to his first All-Star Team.

As Bautista's home run tally rose, the inevitable question came up: Was he using performance-enhancing drugs? But the rumours were not backed up by a shred of evidence. Bautista gave much of the credit to Gaston and Jays' hitting coach Dwayne Murphy, who helped him start his swing earlier and attack the ball more aggressively.

Perhaps frustrated by the steroid accusations, Bautista showed a fiery side on August 23. He welcomed Yankees' rookie Ivan Nova with home run number 39, a monster shot in the third inning to put Toronto up 2–1. When Bautista came to bat again in the sixth with the score tied, Nova threw a pitch near his head and both benches cleared. Bautista got his revenge two innings later by blasting his 40th into the second deck to give the Blue Jays a 3–2 win. He took a good 30 seconds to round the bases.

Bautista collected his 48th long ball at Fenway Park on September 17 to set a new franchise record, and he hit number 49 the next night. The Jays then returned to Toronto for a series against the Mariners and faced eventual Cy Young winner Felix Hernandez. In the first inning of that game, Bautista launched a deep drive to left field for his historic 50th home run.

While his bat made the headlines in 2010, Bautista also proved himself a first-rate defensive player. He

started 45 games at third base, where he wielded a slick glove, and in the outfield he showcased one the most feared arms in the game: he cut down 12 baserunners in 2010, tied for second in the league despite playing only 113 games in the outfield. In both 2009 and 2010, he led the American League in outfield assists per nine innings.

While sluggers like Ryan Howard and Jim Thome have power to all fields, Bautista's home run pattern is freakishly consistent. He hits virtually everything to left and left center. When he came to bat in the ninth inning on September 30, 2010, Bautista had never hit an opposite-field home run in his career. He promptly lined one over the wall in right at Minnesota's Target Field for his 54th and final home run of a magnificent season. It was as if Jose Bautista was trying to prove he really can do it all.

$ 24.95
GATE 55
SECTION FIELD
SEAT A53
G23SH29
06JULY11

CAREER HIGHLIGHTS

- won the AL home run title in 2010 with 15 more long balls than his closest rival, the largest margin since 1956
- awarded the Silver Slugger and Hank Aaron Award in 2010
- selected to the AL All-Star Team in 2010

19 RIGHT FIELD

Jose BAUTISTA

jason BAY

NEW YORK METS ◆ NL East

British Columbia is the center of the logging industry in Canada, but in Trail, B.C., the only lumber that matters is the bat wielded by Jason Bay.

The town of Trail (population 8,000) has sent at least nine players to the National Hockey League, but it wasn't until 2004 that the Bay family put their hometown on the baseball map: Jason's sister Lauren was a pitcher for Canada's Olympic softball team that summer, while her big brother won Rookie of the Year honors in the National League.

The 2004 campaign started late for Jason Bay. He had shoulder surgery in the offseason, and, as a result, didn't join the Pittsburgh Pirates until May. He quickly made up for lost time: he belted 26 home runs (a club record for rookies) and led all NL first-year players in homers, RBIs, slugging, total bases and extra-base hits. Bay's sophomore season in 2005 was even better, as he improved to .306 with 32 homers, 110 runs scored and 101 RBIs. He also demonstrated the good instincts that managers like to see in young ballplayers. With only average speed he swiped 21 consecutive bases (then a major-league record), and his patience at the plate resulted in 95 walks, pushing his on-base percentage over .400. Those positive numbers put a silver lining on his 142 strikeouts.

The 2006 All-Star Game was played at PNC Park in Pittsburgh, and Pirates fans were eager to see one of their own in the starting lineup. Bay helped his own

case with a marvelous May, during which he hit 12 home runs, including going deep in six straight games. That performance helped him finish second in fan voting, trailing only Albert Pujols, and he started the game in right field and batting cleanup.

Bay would go on to have another fine season in 2006, with 35 homers and 109 RBIs, before an off-year the following season. He toiled with the lowly Pirates until just before the trading deadline in 2008, when the Boston Red Sox acquired him in a three-team deal that sent Manny Ramirez to the Dodgers. Back home in Trail, Bay's family was thrilled. His dad is a long-time Red Sox fan, and Jason had grown up with pictures of Jim Rice and Carl Yastrzemski on his bedroom wall. Now he would be patrolling left field in the shadow of the Green Monster.

Bay thrived in Fenway Park, and in 49 games with the Red Sox in 2008, he batted .293 with nine home runs to help the team secure the

AL wild card. Having spent most of his career with a perennial cellar dweller, Bay relished playing in his first postseason, batting .341 with three homers and nine RBIs in 11 games. He just missed his goal of making it to the World Series, however, when the Red Sox lost a tough seven-game ALCS against the Tampa Bay Rays.

The left fielder earned his first Silver Slugger in 2009 with his strongest season yet. He set new career highs with 36 home runs and 119 RBIs, leading the Red Sox in both categories and helping Boston to another postseason berth. But when his contract expired at the end of the season, Bay filed for free agency and signed with the New York Mets.

After struggling with the bat for the first four months of the 2010 season, Bay made a spectacular running catch on July 23 and ran headlong into the left-field fence at Dodger Stadium. He played the next two games, but was diagnosed with post-concussive syndrome and sidelined for the rest of the season. His return to form will be an important factor in helping the Mets become contenders in the tough National League East.

$ 24.95
GATE 18
SECTION CLUB
SEAT D38
L1KB449
18JUNE11

CAREER HIGHLIGHTS

- only Pirate to combine a .300 average with 30 homers, 40 doubles, 100 runs, 100 RBIs and 20 stolen bases in the same season (2005)

- represented Canada at the World Baseball Classic in 2006 and 2009

- named to the NL All-Star Team in 2005 and 2006, and to the AL All-Star Team in 2009

44 LEFT FIELD

Jason BAY

ryan
BRAUN

When the Milwaukee Brewers opened spring training in 2007, Ryan Braun wasn't expected to make the team. Although the club's regular third baseman, Corey Koskie, was sidelined with an injury (which eventually ended his career), the Brewers still felt Braun needed a year in Triple-A to gain more experience, especially on defense. Those plans lasted all of 47 games. By the end of May, Ryan Braun was not only Milwaukee's starting third baseman, he was on his way to becoming one of the most feared sluggers in the game.

Braun grew up in Los Angeles and attended the University of Miami, where he starred as a shortstop. His family must have been amused in 2005 when he was drafted by the Brew Crew — Braun's mother works for the beer maker Anheuser-Busch.

The young infielder raced through the Milwaukee farm system, and seven weeks into the 2007 season it was clear that Braun was ready for the majors. Craig Counsell and Tony Graffanino were platooning at third and batting .231 and .187 respectively, while Braun was tearing up the Pacific Coast League with a .342 average,

.701 slugging percentage and 10 home runs in only 117 at-bats. He debuted with the Brewers on May 24 and immediately showed he belonged with the big boys. In his third at-bat, he drove in a run with a sacrifice fly off future Hall of Famer Greg Maddux. Later in the game, he collected an RBI double for his first big-league hit.

What Braun accomplished during the rest of the season was mind-blowing. He batted .382 in June, then followed with a .345 average and 11 home runs in July. Batting ahead of Prince Fielder, Braun helped the Brewers become surprise contenders in 2007. He finished at .324 with 34 home runs and 97 RBIs in only 113 games. His slugging percentage of .634 not only led the National League, but set a major-league record for rookies. Despite playing only two-thirds of the season, he edged out Troy Tulowitzki in the voting for NL Rookie of the Year.

The Brewers shifted Braun to left field for the 2008 season, a difficult adjustment for a player who had been an infielder throughout his early career. But Braun's strong throwing arm, excellent speed and hard work

CAREER HIGHLIGHTS

- one of only two players in MLB history to hit 30 or more home runs in each of his first three seasons
- two-time Silver Slugger winner (2008–09)
- starting outfielder on the NL All-Star Team 2008–2010

8   LEFT FIELD

Ryan BRAUN

helped him play the entire season without an error. At the plate, he showed no signs of the sophomore jinx. He had another red-hot July, batting .366 with 9 home runs and 23 RBIs and was rewarded with a spot in the starting lineup of the All-Star Game at the old Yankee Stadium.

Braun was magnificent down the stretch, as the 2008 Brewers looked to earn a spot in the postseason for the first time in 26 years. On September 25, he hit a walk-off grand slam in the 10th inning to keep the team's hopes alive. It came down to the last day of the season, with Milwaukee needing a win against the first-place Cubs to earn the wild card spot. With the score tied 1–1 in the bottom of the eighth, Braun came to the plate with a man on and promptly belted the first pitch over the wall in left field for a game-winning homer.

While the Brewers faltered in the playoffs that year, Braun emerged as the team's biggest offensive threat with 37 home runs, 106 RBIs and a league-leading 83 extra-base hits.

Although pitching woes prevented Milwaukee from contending in 2009 and 2010, Braun just kept getting better. Always a home-run threat, he's also a consistent .300 hitter (he smacked a league-leading 203 hits in 2009) and can even be counted on for 15 or 20 stolen bases. The transplanted third baseman is now an outstanding left fielder, too: he topped the league in putouts in each of his three seasons at the position.

Both on and off the field, Braun carries himself with a confident swagger that rubs some people the wrong way, and he and some of his twentysomething teammates clashed with Brewers' manager Ken Macha, whose style was more old-school. With Macha gone after the 2010 season, Ryan Braun has an opportunity to become a leader on an exciting young ball club that's loaded with potential.

shin-soo CHOO

CLEVELAND INDIANS ◆ AL Central

Considering what Shin-Soo Choo can do with his bat, his glove and his legs, it may come as a surprise to learn that scouts were originally interested in his arm.

Choo was born in Busan, South Korea's second largest city, and in his teen years he was a two-time MVP in the country's most prestigious high-school baseball tournament — as a pitcher. In 2000, he pitched for Korea in the World Junior AAA Baseball Championship, and led his country to a gold medal, striking out 33 batters in the tournament. That August, the Seattle Mariners signed Choo as a free agent, and the 18-year-old moved to Arizona to play Rookie ball. The Mariners immediately ended Choo's pitching career by converting him to an outfielder.

By 2005, Choo had worked his way up to Triple-A (in Tacoma in the Pacific Coast League), and that same year he broke into the majors. But the Mariners never gave Choo much playing time, and in the middle of the 2006 season they dealt him to the Cleveland Indians. Two days after the trade, Choo made his debut with the Tribe in a game against his former team. He sent a message by blasting a sixth-inning home run off Felix Hernandez that stood up as the only tally in a 1–0 Cleveland victory.

The Indians put Choo in the lineup as their everyday right fielder in the final two months of 2006, and he responded by batting a solid .295. But the following season was a challenge for the young right fielder. He played only half a dozen games for the Indians in April before being sent back to Triple-A, and then spent two months on the DL with an elbow injury that eventually required Tommy John surgery. That kept him on the sidelines until the following May.

Once Choo returned to the Tribe in 2008, there was no looking back. After the All-Star break he batted .343 with 50 runs scored, 20 doubles and 11 home runs in 58 games, finishing the year with a .309 average

and a .549 slugging percentage. His huge second half set the stage for the role he would play for the Indians over the next two seasons.

Before the start of the 2009 MLB schedule, Choo competed for South Korea in the World Baseball Classic. His three-run bomb in the semifinal against Venezuela led South Korea to a 10–2 victory, but his club eventually lost in the final to Daisuke Matsuzaka and Japan.

Choo's 2009 and 2010 campaigns were remarkably consistent. In his first full season in the bigs, he was the only American League player to bat .300, hit 20 home runs and steal 20 bases, and he became the Indians' most dangerous hitter since the decline of Travis Hafner. Choo reached those same milestones again in 2010, in addition to leading all AL outfielders with 14 assists, showcasing the arm that had once led Busan High School in South Korea to a pair of national championships.

Despite his outstanding numbers, Choo mostly flies under the radar in North America, largely because he plays for a team that has struggled mightily since winning the AL Central in 2007. Back home in South Korea, however, Choo is a national hero. His country

has produced only one truly outstanding player (pitcher Chan Ho Park), and Choo is already the most accomplished Korean-born hitter to wear an MLB uniform.

At the end of the 2010 season, Choo faced a potentially career-ending situation. South Korean men must perform military service by the time they turn 30 years old, so it looked like the 28-year-old might have to put his MLB career on hold just as he was hitting his prime. One option was to apply for U.S. citizenship, but that might mean that Choo would never be allowed to return to his native country. There was also another possibility: if South Korea were to win the gold medal in baseball at the 2010 Asian Games, all members of the team would be rewarded with an exemption from military service. The Indians cleared him to play in the tournament that November, and Choo was magnificent. In five games he batted .571 with 3 home runs (including one in the semifinal against China), 8 runs, and 11 RBIs, as South Korea went undefeated and won the gold.

Now free from compulsory military service, Choo can be sure that the only uniform he'll wear for the next several years is a baseball uniform.

$ 24.95

GATE 12

SECTION UPPER

SEAT AD2

G3RS623

13OCT11

CAREER HIGHLIGHTS

- three consecutive seasons with an average of .300 or better (2008–10)
- only Asian-born member of the 20–20 club, accomplishing the feat in both 2009 and 2010
- led South Korea to a gold medal at the 2010 Asian Games

17 RIGHT FIELD

Shin-Soo CHOO

carl CRAWFORD

BOSTON RED SOX ◆ AL East

CAREER HIGHLIGHTS

- only player in MLB history to reach 100 homers, 100 triples and 400 steals before age 30
- led AL in stolen bases four times from 2003–07
- four-time AL All-Star (2004, 2007, 2009, 2010)

$ 24.95
GATE 32
SECTION FIELD
SEAT SD03
V3SE638
2JUNE11

13 LEFT FIELD

Carl CRAWFORD

Carl Crawford had a lot of distractions growing up. Born in Houston in 1981, he was raised by his mother in the Fifth Ward, a neighborhood rife with poverty, drugs and gangs. But with the encouragement of his mom and his uncle, Jack Crawford — who had played in the California Angels' system — young Carl stayed out of trouble by focusing on sports. In his senior year at Jefferson Davis High School, he was an All-State quarterback in football and a star point guard on the basketball team, while batting .563 on the diamond. He received scholarship offers from Nebraska (football) and UCLA (basketball), but decided to sign with Tampa Bay when they drafted him 52nd overall in 1999 and handed him a $1.2-million bonus.

The Tampa Bay Rays of that era were a dreadful team, and the club was anxious to give the fans something to cheer about. So they rushed the 20-year-old Crawford into the big leagues in July 2002, and he quickly showed a glimpse of the hitter he would soon become. In his first 21 games he smacked five triples, showing off his line-drive power backed up with blazing speed. Crawford's performance that year earned him the full-time job as the team's left fielder and leadoff hitter for 2003.

Crawford's OBP was below average in his first few seasons, but when he did reach first base, he wasted little time getting to second. In his first full season, he led the AL with 55 stolen bases, and then bested that total the following year with a team-record 59 thefts. In 2004 he was rewarded with a chance to play in his first All-Star Game, held at Minute Maid Field in Houston, a short drive from where he grew up.

No one could accuse Crawford of complacency during his early years. He improved his batting average and home-run totals every season from 2002 through 2006, joining Hall of Famer Rogers Hornsby as the only other player to accomplish that feat five years running. While he excelled as a leadoff hitter and base stealer, he also demonstrated legitimate home-run power, not to mention a remarkable talent for three-base hits: Crawford has led the league in triples four times, currently leads all active players, and is a legitimate threat to reach the top 10 all-time.

By 2008, Crawford was coming off his best year to date (.315, 11 homers and a league-best 50 steals), and his team's prospects were looking up as the season opened. The Rays didn't disappoint, and Crawford was a big part of the team's first season as a contender — until early August. That's when he damaged a tendon in his hand and it looked like he might never see a playoff series after all. He missed 46 games, but returned in the final week as the Rays wrapped up the AL East title. In his first postseason, Crawford batted .345 in the ALCS against the Red Sox, including going 5-for-5 in Game 4, as the Rays took a commanding 3–1 lead in the series. When the Rays advanced to the World Series he slugged two home runs, but Philadelphia pitching shut down Crawford and his club the rest of the way.

There seems to be no stopping Carl Crawford. While the Rays had a disappointing campaign in 2009, their left fielder topped the .300 mark for the fourth time and set new personal bests with a .364 OBP and 60 stolen bases. Then he outdid himself in 2010 establishing new career-highs: 19 home runs, 110 runs scored, 90 RBIs and a .495 slugging percentage, and earning his first Silver Slugger Award. He also finally gained recognition for his vast range in left field with his first Gold Glove.

As happens with so many great players in small markets, Carl Crawford became too big for Tampa Bay. His contract with the Rays expired after the 2010 campaign and he signed with the Boston Red Sox during the offseason.

andre ETHIER

LOS ANGELES DODGERS ◆ NL West

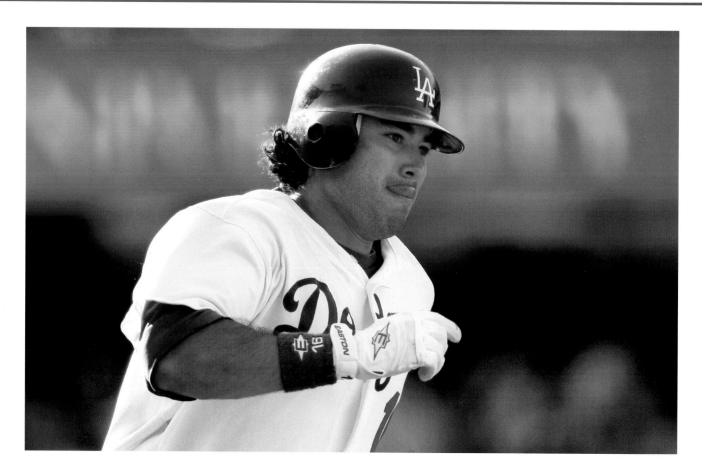

These days, no one strides to the plate in the late innings with more confidence than Andre Ethier. The Dodgers' slugging right fielder has earned a reputation as the game's best clutch hitter, thanks to a remarkable 11 walk-off hits in the past three seasons, more than twice as many as any other player.

Born and raised in Phoenix, Ethier played at Arizona State University, on a team that also included Dustin Pedroia and Ian Kinsler. There he caught the attention of the Oakland Athletics' scouts, who were following general manager Billy Beane's system of identifying players with good pitch selection and high OBPs. The A's selected Ethier in the second round of the 2003 draft.

The outfielder soon became one of the top prospects in the Oakland system, winning the Double-A Texas League Player of the Year award in 2005. A job with the A's seemed inevitable, but in the offseason Oakland sent Ethier to the Dodgers in exchange for Milton Bradley and utility man Antonio Perez. It was one of Beane's worst trades. The troubled Bradley had one decent season with the A's, while Perez was out of the majors within a year. Meanwhile, Ethier helped the Dodgers to three playoff appearances in his first four campaigns.

Ethier made his MLB debut with the Dodgers in front of family and friends in his hometown of Phoenix in May 2006. Later that month he went 5-for-5 in a game against the Angels and went on to bat .344 in

June, and .362 with five homers in July. But the rookie struggled terribly in the final month of the season, and when the Dodgers captured the wild card, Ethier saw only one at-bat in the postseason.

While 2007 was disappointing for the Dodgers (they finished fourth), Ethier earned a lot of playing time, starting 117 games in the outfield. He was also garnering a reputation as a dangerous pinch-hitter. He went 5-for-10 off the bench with two home runs — one tied the game in the eighth, while the other was a three-run blast that won it in the ninth.

When manager Joe Torre arrived in L.A. in 2008, he hired former Yankee superstar Don Mattingly as the team's new hitting coach. Mattingly helped Ethier hone his smooth, left-handed swing, and the outfielder had a breakout season, batting .305 and slugging .510 (both are still career highs). He also popped 20 homers to lead the team, and nine of them came in a three-week span starting in mid-August to help a Dodgers club that was locked in a tight battle for first place. Twice that August he delivered game-winning hits in the bottom of the ninth.

Ethier cemented his reputation as Mr. Clutch in 2009, when he worked his magic in back-to-back games against the Phillies. On June

5, with the Dodgers down 3–2, Ethier smacked a two-out, bases-loaded double in the bottom of the ninth to win the game. The following day, with two outs in the 12th, he launched a walk-off homer to center field. He finished the season with six walk-off hits, four of them home runs to tie an MLB mark last reached in 1957. Overall, he belted 31 homers and became the first left-handed hitter to hit 20 long balls at Dodger Stadium. He rounded out an outstanding year with 42 doubles and 106 RBIs.

The Dodgers fell below .500 in 2010, but not before Ethier treated fans to more late-inning heroics. Having already collected the 10th walk-off hit of his career in April, he came to bat on May 6 with the bases loaded and the game tied 3–3 in the ninth. As the *Los Angeles Times* later said, "Ethier might as well have come to the plate wearing a red cape and with a giant 'S' across the front of his jersey." Almost inevitably, he took a 2–2 pitch and sent it way over the center field wall for a walk-off grand slam.

A week later, batting .392 with 11 home runs, Ethier broke his finger and missed two weeks. He struggled after his return from the DL, but still managed to finish the season with a .292 average and 23 home runs. It's a good bet his numbers would have been even better if all of his at-bats came in the ninth inning.

$ 24.95
GATE 65
SECTION UPPER
SEAT A26
S6SS474
150CT11

CAREER HIGHLIGHTS

- his six walk-off hits in 2009 was the most by any player in 35 years
- won a Silver Slugger Award in 2009
- starting center fielder on the 2010 NL All-Star Team

16 RIGHT FIELD

Andre ETHIER

josh HAMILTON

32

When the PA announcer read out the starting lineups before Game 1 of the 2010 World Series, it was a small miracle that Josh Hamilton was among the names. The Rangers' center fielder wasn't just grateful to be playing in his first Fall Classic. After a decade that saw him go from baseball's top prospect to a desperate drug addict, Hamilton was lucky to be alive.

When the Tampa Bay Rays selected him as the number-one pick out of high school in 1999, they noted that it wasn't just Hamilton's athletic ability that had attracted them. It was also his exceptional character. The churchgoing 18-year-old from Raleigh, North Carolina, was so close with his parents that they quit their jobs to travel with him in the minor leagues.

Then Hamilton's world fell apart. On the way home from a spring training game with his mom and dad in 2001, a dump truck ran a red light and slammed into their pickup. His mother was badly hurt, and both parents returned home to recover from their injuries. Josh, who had suffered a back injury in the crash, stayed in Florida to start the season with the Double-A Orlando Rays. He batted .180 in 23 games before going on the disabled list.

Hamilton's sore back wasn't the only reason his play was suffering. Alone for the first time at age 20, he started hanging around a local tattoo parlor and began using drugs and alcohol for the first time. The next year he was back in Class-A ball, and soon found himself out of baseball altogether, having burned through most of his $3.96 million signing bonus. The player who was once considered a can't-miss prospect played no baseball for more than three years.

One night, after Hamilton had hit rock bottom, he had a dream in which he fought with the devil. The next day he resolved to take back his life — he knew that if he didn't get clean, he would soon wind up dead. It was October 6, 2005.

CAREER HIGHLIGHTS

- two-time Silver Slugger Award winner (2008, 2010)
- won ALCS MVP and AL MVP in 2010
- selected to the AL All-Star Team 2008–2010

32 CENTER FIELD

Josh HAMILTON

Hamilton got the help he needed to give up the drugs and alcohol, though the Rays no longer wanted any part of him. Neither did anyone else. In 2006 Tampa Bay placed him on waivers, where any team could have picked him up for $20,000. No one did.

Later that year, however, the Cincinnati Reds decided to give Hamilton a chance at redemption. After he proved himself in training camp, he earned a spot on the 2007 Opening Day roster, and on April 10 collected his first hit: a game-tying two-run homer. The 25-year-old rookie played 90 games for the Reds that year and hit .292 with 19 home runs.

The Reds were rich with outfielders, however, so in the offseason they dealt Hamilton to the Texas Rangers, where he continued his amazing comeback. Playing every day in center field, he blasted 21 homers and drove in 95 runs in the first half of the season, earning a spot on the AL All-Star Team. He finished the season with a .304 average, 32 long balls and a league-leading 130 RBIs.

Hamilton had a difficult year in 2009. In spring training, after more than three years of being sober, he got drunk in an Arizona bar. Then he missed half the season with bruised ribs and a torn abdominal muscle that needed surgery. But the Rangers stood behind him, and he returned in 2010 with his best season yet, helping Texas build an insurmountable lead in the AL West. When they wrapped up the division, Hamilton celebrated on the field with his teammates, but excused himself from the champagne-popping ritual because he still cannot be around alcohol.

Hamilton's first postseason series was against the Tampa Bay Rays, the team that had drafted him a decade earlier. His first playoff match came on October 6, 2010 — the fifth anniversary of the day he turned his life around. When the Rangers disposed of the Rays in the ALDS, they celebrated with ginger ale. They did it again after knocking off the Yankees in the ALCS to win the pennant. The baffled New York pitchers walked him eight times, but he still smacked four homers and drove in seven runs to win series MVP honors.

Like the rest of his teammates, Hamilton was shut down by San Francisco's pitching staff in the World Series. But he led the majors with a .359 average, a .633 slugging percentage and an OPS of 1.044 and easily won the American League MVP Award. The number-one draft pick who had almost destroyed his life was finally on top of the baseball world.

matt HOLLIDAY

7

No one can accuse Matt Holliday of not paying his dues. While at Oklahoma State University, Holliday looked to be headed for stardom as a quarterback, so MLB teams passed him over again and again in the 1998 draft, until the Colorado Rockies finally grabbed him in the seventh round. The teenager was powerful and deeply committed, but he was inconsistent in the minors, and he toiled away in the Rockies' system for more than six years. Other than his first year at the lowly rookie level, he never hit higher than .276, and he averaged just 11 homers a season. It looked as though he might never blossom into a big leaguer.

Then, at 24 years of age, in 2004, Holliday finally worked his way up to Triple-A, and after just six games he was called up when injuries left two gaping holes in the Rockies' outfield. He surprised everyone with solid numbers in his rookie season: a .290 average, 31 doubles and 14 homers in 400 at-bats.

$ 24.95
GATE 14
SECTION CLUB
SEAT K9
S3TC367
9MAY11

CAREER HIGHLIGHTS

- MVP of the National League Championship Series in 2007
- won four Silver Slugger Awards (2006–08, 2010)
- four-time NL All-Star (2006–08, 2010)

7 LEFT FIELD

Matt HOLLIDAY

Assured a spot in the starting lineup, Holliday started slowly in 2005, and then suffered a broken finger that landed him on the DL for almost six weeks. After returning in late July, however, he batted .323 and popped 15 home runs. In September he piled up a league-leading 32 RBIs, eight of them coming in one game.

Holliday's breakout season came in 2006, when he established himself as one of the best-hitting corner outfielders in the game. Finally showcasing the power that everyone knew he had, Holliday was second in the NL in extra-base hits (84) and fifth in slugging (.586). He batted .326 and belted 34 home runs to go along with 114 RBIs and 119 runs scored, good enough for his first Silver Slugger Award. While he benefited from the hitter-friendly dimensions of Coors Field, a couple of tape-measure homers that season proved that his power was genuine. His longest drive at home traveled an estimated 478 feet, and he launched another in Los Angeles that almost exited Dodger Stadium.

In 2007, Holliday's season had MVP written all over it: he won the batting title (.340) and led the league with 216 hits, 50 doubles, 92 extra-base hits, 386 total bases and 137 RBIs. (However, in the MVP voting, he ended up a close second behind the Phillies' charismatic Jimmy Rollins, who had a career year.) During the stretch drive, Holliday was a monster. In mid-September, he mashed 11 homers and drove in 21 runs in 12 games. In the last dozen matches he batted .457 as the Rockies went 11–1 to force a one-game

playoff against the Padres. In that thrilling tiebreaker, Holliday ripped a game-tying triple off Trevor Hoffman in the 13th inning, and then raced home on a sacrifice fly to score the winning run with a dramatic head-first slide that almost knocked him out. He then led his club to its first World Series appearance with five homers and 10 RBIs in 11 postseason games.

After another fine year with Colorado in 2008 (.321, a career-high .409 OBP and 28 stolen bases), Holliday was dealt to Oakland in a blockbuster deal so the Rockies could acquire closer Huston Street and Carlos Gonzalez. With the slugger set to become a free agent after the 2009 season, it was likely that he'd be in Oakland for only one year, but it turned out to be just 93 games. The A's sent him back to the National League in July in a trade with the St. Louis Cardinals.

Holliday was a welcome addition to the Redbirds. He batted .353 with 13 homers and 55 RBIs to help the Cardinals go 39–26 after the trade. That was good enough to win the NL wild card, and Holliday found himself back in the postseason. In Game 2 of the NLDS against the Dodgers, he hit a home run to open the scoring, but with the Cards leading 2–1 with two outs in the ninth, he lost a fly ball in the lights, and the Dodgers rallied back to win the game and the series.

In his first full campaign with the Cardinals in 2010, Holliday had another All-Star season, batting over .300 for the sixth year in a row and posting his fourth 100-RBI campaign. Matt Holliday may have been a late bloomer, but it looks like his career has deep roots.

torii
HUNTER

48

Torii Hunter traveled a difficult road to the big leagues. Born into poverty in Pine Bluff, Arkansas, he remembers days with no electricity, and having to hide when bill collectors knocked on the door. His biggest motivation for getting to the majors was the promise of earning enough money to help his family.

Hunter was selected by the Minnesota Twins in the first round of the 1993 draft. He struggled with the bat in the minors, but established himself as a magnificent center fielder — during one game in Double-A, he ran right through the plywood fence to catch a would-be home run. He was on the Twins' roster for all of 1999, but after spending half of 2000 in Triple-A, he began to wonder whether he'd ever make it as a full-time major leaguer.

The answer came in 2001. That year Hunter led the Twins with 27 home runs and was second with 92 RBIs. He was also dazzling in the outfield, making an incredible 460 putouts (still a career high) and gunning down 14 runners. That performance won him his first Gold Glove and guaranteed him a spot in the everyday lineup.

It wasn't easy to patrol center field in Minnesota in those days — and not only because balls sometimes struck the Metrodome's Teflon roof, or because the wall in right-center looked and behaved like a giant garbage bag. The toughest part was living with the ghost of Kirby Puckett,

CAREER HIGHLIGHTS

- won nine consecutive Gold Gloves in center field (2001–09)

- has a career .305 average and .489 slugging percentage in eight postseason series

- four-time AL All-Star (2002, 2007, 2009, 2010)

48 RIGHT FIELD

Torii HUNTER

who was beloved by the city from 1984 until he was forced to retire due to glaucoma after the 1995 season. In the post-Puckett era, the revitalized Twins and their fans looked to Torii Hunter to be the new face of the franchise, and he didn't let them down.

In 2002, Hunter was the first Twin to start in an All-Star Game since Puckett seven years earlier, and he wasted no time staking out his territory. In the first inning, Barry Bonds drove a blast to center field that was headed over the wall until Hunter, timing his jump perfectly, leaped and pulled it back. He went on to slug 29 homers and 37 doubles that season as the Twins finished first and defeated the Oakland A's in the ALDS before getting ousted by the Anaheim Angels.

Over the next five seasons, Hunter consistently hit with power, drove in runs and vacuumed up fly balls as he added to his stack of Gold Gloves. He slugged a career-high 31 home runs in 2006, and the following year he smacked 45 doubles and drove in 107 runs, both personal bests. Overall, during Hunter's tenure with the Twins he helped move them from also-rans to perennial contenders who made four trips to the postseason. But although his own playoff numbers were outstanding (in 2003 and 2004 he batted a combined .387 with two homers in eight games), the Twins made three early exits in the ALDS, including two at the hands of the powerhouse Yankees.

As a free agent in November 2007, Hunter

signed a five-year deal with the Los Angeles Angels of Anaheim, where he would anchor an exceptional outfield that included Garret Anderson and Vladimir Guerrero. As it happened, the Angels opened the 2008 season with a four-game series in Minnesota, and Hunter must have felt the pressure. He went 3-for-16, although he did hit a home run in the closer. Hunter went on to reach the 20-homer plateau for the seventh time and played the entire season without an error in center field. The club finished first in the AL West, and despite another solid playoff showing by Hunter (.389 with a team-high 5 RBIs), they were bounced by the Red Sox in the ALDS.

The Angels got their revenge on Boston in the 2009 Division Series when they swept the Sox in three games, thanks in part to a Hunter home run in the opener. But, once again, Hunter found himself in a postseason series with the mighty Yankees, and the result was the same as before: New York eliminated Los Angeles in six games in the ALCS, despite a fine effort (.304) by the center fielder.

Hunter's string of nine consecutive Gold Gloves was finally snapped in 2010, and it's clear that he has lost some speed and range in his mid-30s. His bat, however, remains a potent threat. He batted a career-high .299 in 2009, and has collected 90 RBIs in each of his last two seasons. Los Angeles is an aging ballclub, but they should be able to count on a few more years from this Angel in the outfield.

carlos LEE

45

Only two major-leaguers have hit at least 20 home runs every season since 2000. The first isn't hard to guess: the great Alex Rodriguez has surpassed that milestone annually since 1996. The other is more surprising: the remarkably durable Carlos Lee has belted more than 330 homers and driven in almost 1,200 runs during a 12-year career split between the American and National Leagues.

Lee had already logged five outstanding seasons with the Chicago White Sox when manager Ozzie Guillen took over the team in 2004. He was part of a quintet of sluggers (joining Frank Thomas, Magglio Ordonez, Jose Valentin and Paul Konerko) who hit 20-plus home runs each and powered the team to 95 wins and an AL Central title in 2000. Lee had his best season with the Sox in 2003, collecting 31 dingers and driving in 113 runs.

His 2004 campaign turned out to be just as strong: Lee batted .305 and matched his career high of 31 home runs, established a team record with a 28-game hit streak, and was the only outfielder in the majors to play the whole season without an error. The problem was that Lee had a reputation for dogging it on the base paths and in the outfield. He clashed repeatedly with the hot-headed Guillen, and when the season was over Lee was shipped off to the Milwaukee Brewers.

Lee thrived with his new National League team. He broke a Brewers' club mark in 2005 by driving in 76 runs in the first half — a feat that earned him a

trip to his first All-Star Game — and he finished the season with personal bests in home runs (32) and RBIs (114), winning his first Silver Slugger Award. He had another torrid first half the following year, pounding 26 home runs before the break in 2006. But the Brewers were unable to convince him to agree to a contract extension, and on July 28 they traded him to the Texas Rangers, where he played out the season.

Lee became one of the most sought-after free agents at the end of the 2006 campaign, and while he wouldn't stay in Arlington, he did settle in Texas, signing a six-year contract with the Houston Astros. The Lone Star State suited Lee. He breeds cattle in Aguadulce, Panama, where he was born, and he also owns a ranch outside Houston. While with the White Sox, he picked up the nickname El Caballo (The Horse), and his new cadre of fans at Minute Maid Park took to calling themselves Los Caballitos and rode stick ponies to cheer on the team's slugger. Although the Astros fell to 73–89 in his first year with the club, Lee was one of the bright spots of 2007. He made his third straight All-Star appearance and led the team with 190 hits, 43 doubles and 119 RBIs while batting .303 with 32 home runs.

In his second and third seasons with the Astros, Lee continued to put up big numbers. On August 8, 2008, he reached 100 RBIs for the year and 1,000 in his career, but on the very next day his luck ran out. After dodging the injury bug for years, Lee took a Bronson Arroyo pitch squarely on the little finger, causing multiple fractures that needed surgery to repair. The broken pinky put an end to one of his finest seasons: he had already set career highs in batting average (.314), on-base percentage (.368) and slugging (.569). Healthy again in 2009, he put up more fine numbers, batting an even .300 and leading the Astros with 26 home runs and 102 RBIs. That made it four seasons in a row with an average of at least .300, and eight straight with at least 25 home runs.

Lee had the worst season of his career in 2010, posting a dreary .246 average, though he did manage 24 home runs. His club continued to flounder, as they have done every season since making it to the World Series in 2005. In 2010, the Astros bid adieu to franchise players Lance Berkman and Roy Oswalt and looked to younger talent such as Hunter Pence and J.A. Happ. Like all successful clubs, however, they'll also need leadership from their veterans, and they hope that El Caballo still has some gallop in his step.

$ 24.95
GATE
SECTION **21**
FIELD
SEAT
AA49
D8KA490
18 JUNE 11

CAREER HIGHLIGHTS

- one of only two players to hit 20+ home runs every year since 2000
- leads all MLB outfielders with 852 RBIs since 2003
- three-time NL All-Star (2005–07)

45 LEFT FIELD

Carlos LEE

magglio ORDONEZ

30

W hen the Detroit Tigers signed Magglio Ordonez as a free agent in February 2005, they included an escape clause. The slugging right fielder had strung together five magnificent seasons for the Chicago White Sox, but his 2004 campaign lasted only 52 games because of a knee injury. The Tigers offered $75 million over five years — their biggest free-agent signing to date — but included a condition that would allow them to take back Ordonez's $6 million signing bonus and cancel the deal if their new outfielder spent more than 25 days on the disabled list because of his wonky knee. As it turned out, the Tigers got more than their money's worth from Magglio Ordonez.

Ordonez was born in Caracas, Venezuela, and debuted with the White Sox in 1997. The team's shortstop that year was Ozzie Guillen, a fellow Venezuelan, who would go on to manage the club eight years later. Ordonez's breakout season came in 1999, when he batted .301 with 30 homers and 117 RBIs. He went on to have four more outstanding years in Chicago, during which he averaged 32 homers and slammed 40 or more doubles three times. But when Guillen took over in 2004, he made no secret that he wanted Ordonez gone. The two had never gotten along — they would later describe one another as "enemies" — and the outfielder ended up in Detroit before the 2005 season.

$ 24.95
GATE 24
SECTION FIELD
SEAT C23
S@KJ477
4JULY11

CAREER HIGHLIGHTS

- first AL player to bat .300 with 40 doubles, 30 homers, 100 RBIs and 25 stolen bases in the same season (2001)

- three-time winner of the Silver Slugger Award (2000, 2002, 2007)

- named to the AL All-Star team six times (1999–2001, 2003, 2006, 2007)

30 RIGHT FIELD

Magglio ORDONEZ

Some baseball insiders criticized the Tigers for spending such a huge sum on an injured player who looked to be past his prime. As it turned out, Ordonez's knee was fine. Unfortunately, just three games into his first season in Detroit, he suffered a sports hernia and didn't play again until July. While he wound up batting .302 in 82 games, it was the White Sox who had the last laugh: Ordonez's former team swept the Houston Astros in the 2005 Fall Classic, and his replacement in right field, Jermaine Dye, was World Series MVP.

The tables turned the following season. A healthy Ordonez hit 24 homers and posted his first 100-RBI year since 2002, helping the Tigers win 95 games and the AL wild card. What Detroit fans remember most about 2006 is what Ordonez did in the final game of the ALCS against Oakland. Having already homered to tie the game in the sixth, he came to bat against A's closer Huston Street in the bottom of the ninth. With two out, two on and the score knotted at threes, he took a 1–0 fastball and launched a rainbow shot over the left-field wall to send the Tigers to their first World Series since 1984.

Now settled in Detroit, Ordonez had a career year in 2007. He smacked a league-high 54 doubles and won his first batting title with a .363 average, the highest by a Tiger since Hall of Famer Charlie Gehringer hit .371 way back in 1937. He added 28 home runs and a career-high 139 RBIs, second only to Alex Rodriguez.

Indeed, it was only A-Rod's phenomenal performance in 2007 that prevented Ordonez from copping the MVP award.

On April 22, 2008, Ordonez belted a solo home run to collect career RBI number 1,000, and he finished that campaign with 103, as well as a .317 batting average. He started the 2009 season sluggishly, but he had the hottest hand in the league after the All-Star break, hitting .375 in the second half, including a torrid .439 after September 1. He finished the year at .310 to become the first Tiger since the 1950s to post three consecutive seasons over .300.

Sporting a new look in 2010 — he trimmed his trademark curly black locks — Ordonez started strong and had already surpassed his previous season's home run and RBI totals on July 25 when the Tigers met the Blue Jays at Comerica Park. In that game, Ordonez tried to score from second on a Miguel Cabrera double and caught his right ankle while sliding into home. While it originally looked like he would be out no more than eight weeks, the fracture later required surgery, and he missed the remainder of the season.

The Tigers elected not to exercise their option for 2011, and Ordonez became one of the most sought after free agents in the offseason. But then the outfielder surprised everyone by re-signing with the Tigers, inking a one-year deal for $10 million. This time the contract had no escape clause.

alfonso SORIANO

CHICAGO CUBS ◆ NL Central

Alfonso Soriano has patrolled the outfield since 2006, but he carries the blood of a middle infielder. He was born in San Pedro de Macoris, a town in the Dominican Republic nicknamed "the shortstop factory." At just 19 years old, he began his career in Japan — at shortstop, naturally — before being acquired by the Yankees. New York wasn't about to displace Derek Jeter, however, so they groomed Soriano as a second baseman.

Everyone knew he could run, and his 43 steals in 2001 set a Yankees record for rookies. But Soriano also showed more pop in his bat than your average second baseman, as he slugged 18 homers and drove in 73 runs that year. In the postseason, he belted a ninth-inning jack to beat the Mariners in Game 4 of the ALCS, and added another walk-off hit in the 12th

inning of Game 5 in the World Series.

Soriano was just warming up. The next year he moved to the leadoff spot and batted .300 with 39 home runs, 102 RBIs and a league-leading 209 hits, then followed that up with 38 homers and 91 RBIs in 2003. With more than 35 steals in each season, Soriano was a rare combination of power and speed.

Before the 2004 campaign, the Yankees sent Soriano to the Texas Rangers in a blockbuster trade to get Alex Rodriguez. The second baseman was a perfect fit in an absolutely power-packed Ranger lineup. This group led the majors with 260 home runs in 2005, including 36 by Soriano, who also collected a career-high 104 RBIs to win his third Silver Slugger Award.

When Soriano moved to the Washington Nationals in 2006, he switched from second base to left field —

albeit reluctantly. (After he refused to play the position in a spring training game, *Sports Illustrated* called him "a selfish, greedy prima donna.") He eventually got comfortable in his new role and wound up having an outstanding year. He led the league with 89 extra-base hits and joined Jose Canseco, Barry Bonds and Alex Rodriguez as the only members of the elite 40–40 club, amassing 46 home runs and 41 stolen bases.

After his monster season with the Nationals, Soriano became a free agent and signed an eight-year, $136-million deal with the Chicago Cubs. His first seasons with Lou Piniella's club were a welcome change: after three years with weak teams, Soriano found himself back with a contender. In 2007, despite being hampered by injuries, he was NL Player of the Month in June (.336, 11 homers, 18 RBIs) and had a red-hot September, pounding 14 home runs, including seven leadoff dingers to set a new MLB mark for a single month. The late surge helped Chicago win the NL Central, but like the rest of the Cubs, Soriano couldn't get it going in the NLDS (he was 2-for-14) and his club bowed out to the Diamondbacks in three straight.

Soriano spent two more stints on the DL in 2008, but still managed 29 home runs and 75 RBIs in 109 games. Three of the long balls came in one September game against the Reds, only the second time in MLB history that a leadoff hitter has hit a trio of homers in one match. Chicago won 97 games and finished atop the NL Central again; but for a second straight year, Soriano and the Cubs made a quick adios in the

postseason — the Dodgers swept them in the NLDS and the left fielder was 1-for-14.

Hobbled by an array of leg injuries, Soriano is no longer a base-stealing threat, and by 2009 he'd moved to sixth in the Cubs' batting order, where he batted just .241. He rebounded in 2010 and played in 147 games (the most action he'd seen since 2006) and led his team with 40 doubles and a .496 slugging percentage. The Cubs, however, fell below .500 for the first time in Soriano's four-year tenure.

In late August 2010, Piniella stepped down as the Cubs' manager and left behind a team of aging superstars whose best years may be behind them, including Aramis Ramirez and Carlos Zambrano. Alfonso Soriano may fit that description, too, but his accomplishments rank him among the greatest second basemen and leadoff hitters of all time.

ichiro
SUZUKI

SEATTLE MARINERS ◆ AL West

I chiro Suzuki's career has included a string of impressive accomplishments, but the most remarkable is this: he is the only player who can claim to be the greatest leadoff hitter of two different decades, on two different continents.

Ichiro — like Madonna, Elvis and other great artists — is instantly recognized by his first name, which he wears on the back of his jersey. In 1994, he became a regular with the Orix Blue Wave of the Pacific League, one of Japan's two premier loops. In his first full season he collected 210 hits and a .385 average, both league records, and he went on to win the Pacific League batting title seven times, as well as seven Gold Gloves for his stellar play in the outfield.

In 2000, the Seattle Mariners paid the Blue Wave $13 million for the right to negotiate with Ichiro, and the following year he became the first Japanese hitting star to play every day in North America. There was no shortage of predictions that Ichiro would fall flat. Being five-foot-nine and slightly built may have been fine in Japan, but could he cut it in the hard-hitting American League?

It didn't take long for him to silence the doubters. Ichiro picked up four hits in the Mariners' opening series in 2001, and the following week he threw a 200-foot bullet from right field to gun down a runner at third base. Some sportswriters said it was the finest throw they had ever seen. (In 2010, *Baseball America* still ranked him as the best outfield arm in the league.) Ichiro's rookie season, in fact, was one of the greatest debuts ever. He won the batting

crown with a .350 average, led the loop with 56 stolen bases, and picked up 242 hits — no one had collected that many since 1930. Ichiro became just the second rookie ever to be named MVP. He also added a Gold Glove and led the majors with more than three million All-Star votes, many from Japanese fans who sent their support via the Internet. Along the way, the Mariners won 116 games to tie the major-league record for most victories.

Ichiro had a record-smashing year in 2004 as he lined, chopped, bunted, blooped and hustled out 262 hits, surpassing George Sisler's mark of 257, which had stood for 83 years. He won his second batting title with a .372 average, tops in the majors. In both 2007 and 2009, he again batted over .350 and was second in the AL both times. While he hasn't won a batting title since 2004, he has led the league in hits every year from 2006 through 2010, with more than 210 every season.

Ichiro does have his detractors. He truly is a singles hitter: during his 262-hit season, only 37 were for extra bases, and of his 2,244 hits as of 2010, 516 never left the infield. He also drives in few runs, even for a leadoff

man. In 2010, Ichiro collected just one RBI for every 17 plate appearances. And, while he rarely strikes out, he walks even less and his on-base percentage is lower than one would expect from someone with a career batting average of .331.

One thing no can say about Ichiro is that he's showing his age. He remains a constant threat to steal even in his late 30s. Not only is Ichiro among the league leaders in thefts, but he's also one of the least likely to get caught. In 2006, he swiped 45 bags while getting thrown out just twice, including a stretch of 39 in a row. Four seasons later, the 36-year-old stole 42 in 51 attempts. He's also the league's best defensive right fielder and has 10 consecutive Gold Gloves to prove it.

In 2010, his tenth season with the Mariners, Ichiro moved to the top of the leader board in a couple of major categories. He collected over 200 hits for the tenth time, passing Ty Cobb and moving into a tie with Pete Rose for the most seasons reaching that milestone. He also tied both Cobb and Rose by leading the majors in hits for the seventh time. Rose collected 4,256 hits in his 24 seasons and is currently the all-time leader. But Ichiro amassed 1,278 safeties during nine seasons in Japan, and if he can maintain his current pace, he will join MLB's 3,000-hit club in 2014. That would make him the most prolific batsman in baseball history.

vernon
WELLS

10

When the Angels' 2011 season opened, the team boasted two of the greatest center fielders of the last decade — and neither one was playing center field. Torii Hunter, owner of nine Gold Gloves, was shifted to right field to make room for the young speedster Peter Bourjos. And making his debut in left was three-time Gold Glover Vernon Wells, who had arrived in Los Angeles in the offseason after a dozen years in Toronto.

From 2002 to 2010, Vernon Wells was the face of the Blue Jays franchise: during a difficult decade, he was the one constant in the lineup. Surprisingly, the center fielder was not the first Vernon Wells to play pro sports in Canada. His dad — also named Vernon — briefly played for the Calgary Stampeders of the Canadian Football League. The family eventually settled in Arlington, Texas, where the elder Vernon, an accomplished sports artist, often visited the Texas Rangers' clubhouse, where he introduced his son to baseball legends such as Rickey Henderson and Reggie Jackson.

Wells excelled in football and baseball during high school, and he decided on the latter when the Blue Jays drafted him fifth overall in 1997. After two years in the minors, Wells jumped from Class-A all the way to the big leagues in 1999 and was the Jays' everyday center fielder in the final month of that campaign. But over the next two seasons, Toronto's talented outfield included Jose Cruz, Shawn Green, Shannon Stewart and Raul Mondesi, and the youngster had

little chance of breaking into that lineup. The 23-year-old finally secured the center fielder's job in 2002 and made it clear he intended on keeping it. In his first full season, Wells socked 23 homers and became the youngest Blue Jay ever to collect 100 RBIs.

That was a sneak preview of Wells' 2003 breakout season, when he pounded out a league-leading 215 hits (still a franchise record), including 49 doubles and 33 home runs, scored 118 runs and drove in 117. Wells was equally brilliant with his glove, and in late August that year, during a game at Fenway Park, he made what may have been the greatest catch of his career. With the Red Sox trailing 7–6, Todd Walker doubled to open the seventh, and one out later Manny Ramirez launched a bomb toward the cavernous "Triangle" in center field, some 420 feet from the plate. Wells raced after the ball and made a spectacular grab just before crashing into the wall. He then made a tremendous throw back to the infield to chase a startled Walker back to second base.

The 2004 season was a disaster for the Blue Jays, who finished last, but Wells was now coming of age in center field. That year, he won the first of three straight Gold Gloves, and the following season he played 156 games without an error and tossed in a career-best 12 assists.

Wells earned his second All-Star selection in 2006 with another outstanding year at the plate. He batted .303 with 32 long balls and 106 RBIs. But his performance took a dive the following season (.245 with just 16 home runs), and he missed more than 50 games to injury in 2008. When he disappointed again in 2009 — his on-base percentage was a dreary .311 and he managed a mere 15 home runs — more than a few Blue Jays fans wondered if the 31-year-old was already in the twilight of his career.

But the 2010 season made it clear that Wells still has a lot more to contribute. He got off to a strong start, batting .337 with eight home runs in April, and then finished the year just as hot — he had clearly regained his power stroke. His 31 homers helped the Blue Jays lead the majors in that category, his .515 slugging percentage was his highest since 2006, and his 44 doubles were his most since leading the league in two-baggers seven years earlier. He also finished the season without a single error.

The strong season caught the attention of the Angels, who acquired Wells in an offseason deal that sent Juan Rivera to Toronto. Although he had never played a single big-league game in left field, Wells graciously accepted the position on his new ball club and looked forward to playing with a contender in Los Angeles. After spending his whole career without a visit to the postseason, Vernon Wells is looking forward to his moment in the sun.

$ 24.95

GATE 8

SECTION FIELD

SEAT G23

A3A22FA 1JUNE11

CAREER HIGHLIGHTS

- third center fielder (after Hall of Famers Joe DiMaggio and Al Simmons) to collect 100 RBIs in his first two seasons
- won three consecutive Gold Gloves (2004–06)
- selected to the AL All-Star Team in 2003, 2006 and 2010

10   LEFT FIELD

Vernon WELLS

chris YOUNG

At six-foot-two with a lanky frame, Chris Young looks more like a speed demon than a power hitter. In fact, he's a bit of both. During his first four seasons with the Arizona Diamondbacks, Young has hit both leadoff and cleanup, showing that he can win games with a stolen base or a home run, not to mention an outstanding glove in center field.

Chris Young grew up in Houston, where he attended Bellaire High School, well known for its outstanding baseball program. Young wasn't his school's regular center fielder until his senior year, however, and even then he was not a highly ranked prospect. During the playoffs in his final high-school season, he broke his forearm badly in a collision with his left fielder, and his hopes for being drafted looked remote. But the Chicago White Sox were prepared to take a chance on Young, and they selected him in the 16th round.

When the arm eventually healed, the skinny outfielder started to make his mark in the minor leagues. He had never been a home-run hitter to that point, but in 2004 he learned to lift the ball and surprised everyone with 24 jacks in Class-A. The following year he was named the organization's top minor-league player after hitting 26 home runs and swiping 32 bases for the Double-A Birmingham Barons.

At the end of the 2005 season, the White Sox sent the 21-year-old to Arizona for pitcher Javier Vazquez, and Young spent 2006 with the Triple-A Tucson Sidewinders, where he had an All-Star season. He made his MLB debut with the Diamondbacks as a late-season call-up that year.

Young was still considered a rookie in 2007, and his freshman year with the Diamondbacks surpassed all expectations. Playing center field and batting mostly in the leadoff spot, Young hit 32 home runs — including nine leading off games, tops in the majors — and stole 27 bases. He smashed the franchise rookie records in those categories, as well as in runs (85), doubles (29),

slugging (.467) and extra-base hits (64). He helped the Diamondbacks win the NL West title and then continued his strong play into the postseason, where his two homers helped Arizona sweep the Chicago Cubs in the NLDS.

In his second full season, Young dropped to 22 home runs, but he lashed 42 doubles and 7 triples, and drove in 85 runs despite batting mostly in the leadoff or number-two spot. He also committed just three errors while patrolling Chase Field's cavernous power alleys.

Young's 2009 season was something of a nightmare. By mid-July, he was batting under .200, and the following month the frustrated and hapless Diamondbacks sent him down to Triple-A to try to find his swing. It seemed to work, because when he returned to the big club he smacked 8 homers and drove in 14 runs during the final month of the season.

Although the Diamondbacks continued their slide in 2010 (they lost 97 games and finished in the NL West cellar

for the second straight year), Young was a bright spot. He was the club's lone representative at the All-Star Game, where he participated in the Home Run Derby and caught the final out in a National League victory. On August 7, he accomplished the rare feat of leading off the game with a home run and then ending it with a walk-off blast — only the fourth time a player had done so in the last 40 years. The statisticians ranked him tops among the league's center fielders in overall range, and he belted 27 home runs and set new career highs in on-base percentage (.341), OPS (.793), runs batted in (91) and stolen bases (28).

Chris Young is never going to win a batting title (his .257 average in 2010 was a career high), and he'll need to cut down on his strikeouts if he's ever going to be an elite hitter. But with a dangerous combination of power, speed and slick defense, he is a player who can attack opponents on many fronts.

$ 24.95
GATE 45
SECTION FIELD
SEAT F12
GARE 162
17OCT11

CAREER HIGHLIGHTS

- first rookie in MLB history to hit 30 home runs and steal 25 bases (2007)

- only the second Diamondback player to join the 20–20 club twice (2007, 2010)

- named to the NL All-Star Team in 2010

CENTER FIELD

24

Chris YOUNG

MIGUEL CABRERA - Detroit Tigers

PRINCE FIELDER - Milwaukee Brewers

RYAN HOWARD - Philadelphia Phillies

DEREK JETER - New York Yankees

PAUL KONERKO - Chicago White Sox

EVAN LONGORIA - Tampa Bay Rays

JUSTIN MORNEAU - Minnesota Twins

DUSTIN PEDROIA - Boston Red Sox

ALBERT PUJOLS - St. Louis Cardinals

HANLEY RAMIREZ - Florida Marlins

BRIAN ROBERTS - Baltimore Orioles

ALEX RODRIGUEZ - New York Yankees

MARK TEIXEIRA - New York Yankees

TROY TULOWITZKI - Colorado Rockies

CHASE UTLEY - Philadelphia Phillies

JOEY VOTTO - Cincinnati Reds

DAVID WRIGHT - New York Mets

RYAN ZIMMERMAN - Washington Nationals

Infield
FLYERS

DETROIT TIGERS ◆ AL Central

Miguel Cabrera experienced a baptism by fastball during his rookie season. The 20-year-old had joined the Florida Marlins midway through the 2003 campaign, and four months later found himself in the World Series. Cabrera walked to the plate in the first inning of Game 4 to face Roger Clemens and swung through two pitches to get behind 1–2. Then the Rocket brushed him back with a high heater, knocking the youngster on his backside. One might have forgiven Cabrera if he felt intimidated. But he got up, fouled off two pitches, and then hit the next one into the right-field seats for a two-run homer. The Marlins went on to win the game, and then took the next two to complete their second World Series championship.

Cabrera first caught the eye of Florida scouts while he was a teenager in Maracay, Venezuela. Although he was a shortstop at the time, the organization began grooming him as a third baseman. By mid-2003, he was batting .365 in Triple-A, and the Marlins decided to see what he could do at the big-league level. The underachieving team had little to lose: on June 18, Florida was 34–39 and in last place in the NL East. Cabrera made his debut two days later, and after going 0-for-4 in the first nine innings, he belted a walk-off homer in the 11th for his first major-league hit. He was soon in the lineup full time, playing the outfield and third base. Cabrera got some big hits down the stretch and helped the Marlins secure the wild card and ride the momentum all the way to the Fall Classic.

Cabrera emerged as the best young hitter in the National League in 2004. As a 21-year-old, he batted .294 and led the club with 33 homers, 112 RBIs, 101 runs, 68 walks and a .512 slugging percentage. He posted more great numbers over the next three years, capturing two Silver Slugger Awards and just missing the NL batting title with a .339 average in 2006.

In 2007, when Cabrera was still just 24, fans, the media, and baseball insiders began to wonder aloud

CAREER HIGHLIGHTS

- youngest player (22 years, 143 days) to have back-to-back seasons with 30 or more home runs (2004–2005)

- seven straight seasons with at least 100+ RBIs and 300+ total bases (2004–2010)

- named to five All-Star Teams with the Marlins (2004–07) and Tigers (2010)

24   FIRST BASE

Miguel CABRERA

whether the young superstar was letting himself go. He was 185 pounds when he hit his dramatic home run in the 2003 World Series, and four years later he was tipping the scales at 250. In his second season at third base, the slow-footed Cabrera led the league with 23 errors. His close friend, White Sox manager Ozzie Guillen, took him aside and told him to shape up or he'd find himself playing in the Mexican League.

That winter, the Marlins dealt Cabrera and pitcher Dontrelle Willis to the Detroit Tigers for a half dozen prospects, and the slugger signed an eight-year deal worth more than $153 million. After two weeks of watching Cabrera play the hot corner, they moved him across the diamond to first base, where he's been a fixture ever since.

In his first year with his new club, Cabrera led the AL with 37 home runs and 331 total bases, and set a career high with 127 RBIs. He started the 2009 season with a bang, going 4-for-6 on Opening Day with six RBIs, including a mammoth grand slam. He went on to bat .324 with 34 homers on the year, the sixth straight in which he drove in over 100 runs. That performance helped the Tigers hold on to first place in the AL Central for most of the year.

But as the Twins closed in during the final weekend of the season, Cabrera found himself in the middle of controversy. He got drunk barely 12 hours before the second-last game and then went 0-for-4, stranding six runners, in a 5–1 Tigers loss. That allowed Minnesota to catch Detroit and force a one-game playoff. Cabrera had two hits in the tiebreaker, including a two-run homer, but the Twins earned the postseason berth by winning the game 6–5 in 12 innings.

Cabrera sought help for his alcohol problem in the offseason and in 2010 he showed no ill effects on the diamond. He had an MVP-caliber season, batting .328 with career highs in home runs (38) and slugging (.622). He led the AL with a .420 on-base percentage and paced the majors with 126 RBIs. He might have had even better numbers, but he sat out the last 12 games when he sprained his ankle lunging toward first base on a pick-off attempt. Those dozen games were the most he's missed in a season since becoming a full-time player in 2004. For all of the concerns about how Cabrera treats his body, he has proven to be as durable and consistent as they come.

prince FIELDER

As home-run hitters go, Prince Fielder has good genes. His father is Cecil Fielder, the two-time American League home-run champion who pounded 51 long balls for the Detroit Tigers in 1990, and then 44 more the following year. Prince often went on the road with his dad and sometimes took batting practice with him. When he was 12 years old, Prince even hit a ball over the right-field fence in the old Tiger Stadium.

The younger Fielder inherited not only his father's home-run power, but also his body type. Cecil's weight eventually derailed his career, and by high school Prince was already over 300 pounds. He worked out hard and dropped a lot of the extra baggage, but his weight was such a concern among scouts that some teams were afraid to touch him when he became eligible for the draft in 2002. The Milwaukee Brewers, however, surprised everyone by taking him seventh overall, even passing over hot prospects like Scott Kazmir and Nick Swisher. Almost 200 home runs later, that choice is looking awfully good.

Fielder lit up pitchers at every minor league level, and after belting 28 homers in Triple-A, he earned a shot with the Brewers in 2005. On June 25, in the sixth inning of a game against the Minnesota Twins, Fielder was called on to pinch-hit with two runners on and the Brewers trailing 5–4. The 21-year-old met the challenge by driving a pitch over the wall in left-center for his first major-league home run, which held up as the game winner.

Fielder earned the starting job at first base in 2006 and went to work immediately, batting .344 in April with 10 multi-hit games, 5 home runs and 16 RBIs to take NL Rookie of the Month honors. Not wanting to be typecast as an all-or-nothing power hitter, Fielder kept his average at .300 or better until June 12 before cooling off in the second half and finishing at .271. He led all NL rookies with 28 home runs and was a bright

spot on a team that finished fourth in its division.

Hardly anyone gave Milwaukee a chance before the 2007 season. But the Brew Crew grabbed hold of first place in the NL Central on April 21 and built their lead as Fielder batted .321 with 13 home runs in May. By the break, the slugger had surpassed his home-run total of the previous year and managed to edge out Albert Pujols, Ryan Howard and Derek Lee as the starting first baseman on the National League All-Star Team. The Cubs eventually overtook the Brewers to win the division, but Fielder crushed 20 homers in the final two months to finish with an even 50 to lead the league. In only his second season, Prince was a home-run king.

The big first baseman's 34 homers and 102 RBIs helped the Brewers to a 90–72 record in 2008, good enough to secure the NL wild card. But Fielder went just 1-for-14 in the postseason (his one hit was a home run) as the Phillies made short work of the Brewers on their way to a World Series championship.

Fielder posted one of the best seasons in franchise history in 2009. He again flirted with 50 home runs (he finished with 46) and became a run-producing machine with 141 RBIs, tied for tops in the league. He also emerged as a more mature hitter: while he still struck out 138 times, he drew 110 walks and batted .299 to finish with an OPS of 1.014, second only to the great Pujols. And while he may never win a Gold

Glove, he improved his defensive play in 2009, committing just seven errors at first base, down from 17 the season before.

As the Brewers endured another subpar season in 2010, Fielder's home-run, slugging and RBI numbers were all down. He batted .233 with runners in scoring position and drove in 58 fewer runs than the year before. When he belted his 30th homer of the season in September, however, he became only the second Brewer ever to have four straight seasons with more than 30 home runs. He also continued to develop his patience at the plate, leading the league with 114 bases on balls and posting a .401 OBP, third-best in the loop.

ryan HOWARD

PHILADELPHIA PHILLIES ◆ NL East

Ryan Howard found himself in a strange predicament at the end of 2004. In 131 minor-league games and 19 more with the Phillies, he had hit 48 homers and driven in 136 runs. Yet despite those huge numbers, there was something blocking his way to becoming a major-league first baseman. That something was Jim Thome, who owned the job in Philadelphia and had hit 42 homers of his own in 2004, and 47 the year before.

Howard is too nice a guy to have wished for something bad to happen to Thome. But as fate would have it, the veteran slugger developed tendinitis in his elbow in July 2005 and was gone for the year. The Phillies called up Howard, who gave his team postseason hopes with a tremendous run down the stretch, including 10 dingers in September, a record for a first-year player. (The Phillies finished one game out in the wild card race.) Though he played just 88 games, Howard amassed 22 homers and drove in 63 runs to win the NL Rookie of the Year Award.

The Phils were so smitten that they traded Thome in the offseason to make room for their young star, and Howard responded with a tremendous first half in 2006. He slammed 28 homers and tallied 71 RBIs before the break, and his second half was even better. He hit a torrid .355 after the All-Star Game and added 30 homers to finish with 58, along with 149 RBIs to lead the majors in both categories. The Cardinals' Albert Pujols also had a huge season, but Howard got 20 of the 32 first-place votes to win the MVP Award in his first full year.

The Phillies scraped into the playoffs on the final day of the 2007 season, but they were quickly swept by the Rockies in the NLDS. The following season, however, Philadelphia won 92 games and looked to go deeper into the postseason. Howard helped get them there by pacing the majors with 48 long balls and 146 RBIs — including 84 before the All-Star break. The first baseman hit just .182 in the Division Series against

CAREER HIGHLIGHTS

- set an all-time record for home runs by second-year players with 58 (2006)
- reached 100 and 200 career home runs faster than any other player
- topped 140 RBIs in 2006, 2008 and 2009, leading the majors in each season

6   FIRST BASE

Ryan HOWARD

the Brewers, but he improved to .300 with a couple of RBIs as Philadelphia took care of the Dodgers in the NLCS. Then he uncorked his power in the World Series against the Tampa Bay Rays. Howard homered in the Phils' 5–4 win in Game 3 and then blasted a pair in a five-RBI performance in the next match. The Phillies took Game 5 as well to win their first World Series since 1980.

The big man reached 45 home runs for the fourth straight season in 2009, set a career high with 37 doubles, and again led the majors in RBIs with 141. On July 16 he reached 200 career homers faster than any player before him (658 games). When Philadelphia won its second straight pennant, Howard had another productive postseason. He set National League records by driving in at least one run in seven straight games and by amassing 17 RBIs overall. His biggest hit came in the deciding game of the NLDS against the Rockies: with the Phillies losing 4–2 and down to their final out, Howard drove a ball off the right-field wall for a game-tying double, then raced around to score the winning run on Jayson Werth's single. On the downside, he also set an MLB mark with 13 strikeouts

in the World Series, as the Phillies bowed out to the Yankees in six games.

Howard's 2010 numbers entered the realm of mere mortals, though he still became the first Philly player to reach 30 homers and 100 RBIs in five straight seasons. The club posted the best record in baseball and breezed past the Reds in the NLDS, but the Giants were too much for them in the Championship Series. Howard took a lot of criticism for his playoff performance. Although he batted .303, he failed to drive in a single run in nine games and struck out 17 times in 38 plate appearances — including the one that ended the Phillies' season, when he was caught looking by Giants' closer Brian Wilson with the tying run at second.

Howard's propensity to strike out remains the biggest knock against his game. He whiffed 199 times in both 2007 and 2008 and has averaged a strikeout every 3.6 at-bats over his career. But he's also shown a willingness to walk (his career OBP is .372) and to shorten his swing and use the whole yard (about half of his home runs are to center field or the opposite field). So far, no one has built a ballpark that can contain Ryan Howard.

derek JETER

2

Derek Jeter isn't a native New Yorker, but he's a homegrown Yankee nonetheless. Jeter was born on the other side of the George Washington Bridge in Pequannock, New Jersey, and his childhood dream was to wear the pinstripes. He was drafted by the Yankees in 1992, and before he turned 22 years old, he was their Opening Day shortstop. Since then — over a period spanning 16 seasons and almost 20,000 innings — he has never fielded any other position.

Jeter's arrival marked the beginning of a dynasty that would see the Yankees win four World Series championships in five years. In his first full season in 1996, he batted .314 and won Rookie of the Year honors. (The team's catcher that year was Joe Girardi, who would take over for Joe Torre as manager in 2008.) Jeter's first playoff home run that year is perhaps still his most famous: with the Yankees trailing Baltimore 4–3 in the eighth inning of Game 1 of the ALCS, Jeter hit a fly ball to deep right field and a 12-year-old boy reached over the fence and caught it. Replays showed the ball would not have cleared the wall without the fan's interference, but the umpires ruled it a game-tying home run, and the Yankees went on to win in extra innings. They eventually finished off the Orioles and the Atlanta Braves for their first World Series championship in 15 seasons.

By 1998, Jeter had evolved into one of the league's best-hitting middle infielders, as he smacked 203 hits, led the loop with 127 runs, and tallied 19 homers to break the club record for shortstops. He did even

- leads all active players with 2,926 career hits

- has played in 30 playoff series and holds MLB records for postseason hits (185), runs (101) and games played (147)

- only shortstop in MLB history to record seven seasons of 200 or more hits

2 SHORTSTOP

Derek JETER

better the following season. After reaching base safely in the first 53 games of 1999, he scored 134 runs, had his first 100-RBI campaign and was the runner-up for the batting title with a .349 average. Jeter earned two more rings when the Yankees steamrolled their way to back-to-back World Series wins in 1998 and 1999, thanks in part to his combined .353 clip in both Fall Classics.

The 26-year-old stroked a single in the final week of 2000 to become the second-youngest Yankee to reach 1,000 hits — only Mickey Mantle was younger. In his third All-Star appearance that year, he went 3-for-3 and was the game's MVP, but he saved his real magic for the postseason. He slugged .864 in the Subway Series against the Mets and was named World Series MVP as the Yankees completed the "three-peat." (Jeter remains the only player to win All-Star Game MVP and World Series MVP in the same season.)

In 2001, Jeter expanded his reputation as a clutch postseason player. His play in Game 3 of the Division Series against Oakland still shows up on Top 10 lists: he ran all the way across the diamond to retrieve an errant throw from right field, and then flipped the ball to catcher Jorge Posada to nail Jeremy Giambi at home. It was one of the most creative plays in playoff history, and it preserved a 1–0 Yankees win and reversed the momentum in the series.

For more than decade, the durable shortstop could be relied on to bat around .300, score over 100 runs and drive in 70 or more from the second spot in the batting order. Jeter's best offensive year came in 2006,

when he batted .343, won his first Silver Slugger and finished second in the AL MVP voting.

At age 35 in 2009, he became the Yankee's everyday leadoff man and filled that role with a .334 average, 18 home runs and 30 stolen bases on his way to winning the Hank Aaron Award as the league's top offensive player. On September 11 that year, he collected his 2,722nd career hit, passing Lou Gehrig to become the Yankees' all-time leader. New York returned to the World Series in 2009 and once again Jeter was a sparkplug. He batted .344 in the postseason, reached base in all 15 games, belted 3 homers and scored 14 runs as he won his fifth championship ring.

Jeter is one of baseball's good guys, the embodiment of maturity and class. He is so well respected for his leadership, in fact, that many fans outside of New York argue that he is overrated as a player, particularly when it comes to defense. Statistical analysts are unanimous in declaring him a below-average shortstop with very limited range, and yet the votes of managers and coaches rewarded Jeter with five Gold Gloves between 2004 and 2010.

Just don't mention any of that criticism to Yankee fans. Derek Jeter is the heart of the most successful baseball team of the last two decades, and what he means to his club can't be measured by statistics.

paul
KONERKO

Paul Konerko's major-league success didn't come as a surprise to anyone. As a catcher he led his high school in Scottsdale, Arizona, to a state championship in 1994 and grabbed the attention of major-league bird dogs. The Los Angeles Dodgers selected him in the first round of the draft that year, and by 1998, *Baseball America* ranked him as the second-best prospect in the game, ahead of Todd Helton, Adrian Beltre and Miguel Tejada.

Konerko had brief tenures with the Dodgers and the Cincinnati Reds, but it wasn't until his first season with the White Sox that he had a chance to fulfill his promise. As a 23-year-old in 1999, he batted .294 with 24 home runs and nailed down the job at first base — one he would hold for more than a decade.

Showing he could hit for average and power, Konerko established himself with a string of three solid seasons, peaking in 2002 when he batted .304 with 27 homers and 104 RBIs. But the 2003 season was not so kind. By the time the Midsummer Classic rolled around, Konerko was hobbling along at .197 with a measly five home runs, and manager Jerry Manuel resorted to benching him.

No one took that performance to heart more than Konerko himself. He has a reputation for being his own harshest critic, constantly going over his mechanics and looking for ways to improve his swing. He obviously fixed the problem, because in 2004 he erupted for a career-best 41 jacks to go along with 117 RBIs and upped his average to .277, good enough to earn AL

Comeback Player of the Year honors.

When Konerko got off to a slow start again in 2005 — he was batting .232 at the end of May — fans and coaches wondered whether he had slipped back into his old habits. But from June 1 to the end of the season, he batted .312 and socked 27 home runs, reaching 40 for the second year in a row. The White Sox, meanwhile, led the AL Central from start to finish, winning 99 games and earning a spot in the postseason for the first time since 2000. Konerko had gone 0-for-9 in the playoffs that year and was looking for redemption. He found it: the slugger homered twice in the Division Series as the White Sox swept Boston in three straight. Then his first-inning homers in Games 3 and 4 in the ALCS paced his team to a decisive win over the Angels and sent the White Sox to their first World Series in 46 years.

In the Fall Classic, Chicago faced the Houston Astros and a pitching staff led by Roger Clemens and Andy Pettitte. The Sox roughed up Clemens in Game 1, but in the seventh inning of Game 2 they were down 4–2, and it looked like the Astros would get back in the series. That's when Konerko came to bat with the bases loaded and two out. He sent reliever Chad Qualls' first pitch into the seats for a grand slam and a 6–4 White Sox lead. Chicago went on to win the game and then took the next two to complete the sweep and clinch their first World Series championship since 1917. Konerko had the honor of making the final putout of all three postseason series.

The big first baseman limped through 2008 with a trio of injuries and his average fell to .240, but he rebounded with another strong year in 2009. One of the highlights of his season came on April 13, when both he and teammate Jermaine Dye entered the game with 299 career home runs. After Dye led off the second inning with a homer to left field to reach the 300 milestone, Konerko stepped to the plate and immediately did the same.

At age 34, Konerko surprised a lot of people with an MVP-caliber season in 2010. He opened the campaign with 11 home runs in April, a club record, and stayed hot all season, finishing second in the league with 39 taters. He set new career highs in OBP (.393), slugging (.584) and total bases (320). He helped the Sox move into first place for much of July and August, but the team's September swoon left them well back of Minnesota.

The White Sox thought they might lose Konerko after his big 2010 season as he shopped around on the free-agent market. But in the end he agreed to re-sign for three years and help Chicago take another run at a championship before his great career is over.

$ 24.95

GATE 29

SECTION CLUB

SEAT E16

G8HT556
3JULY11

CAREER HIGHLIGHTS

- shares White Sox franchise record for most seasons with at least 20 home runs (11)
- won ALCS MVP award in Chicago's 2005 championship season
- selected to the AL All-Star Team four times since 2002

14 FIRST BASE

Paul KONERKO

evan LONGORIA

3

TAMPA BAY RAYS ◆ AL East

The reversal of fortune for the Tampa Bay franchise was remarkably swift. In their first decade after joining the American League, the Devil Rays never failed to lose fewer than 91 games and finished dead last in the East nine times. Before the 2008 campaign, however, the team did more than just drop the "Devil" in its name. The newly christened Tampa Bay Rays emerged as one of baseball's best teams and finished atop MLB's toughest division twice over the next three years. No one has played a bigger role in this transformation than Evan Longoria.

When the Rays' breakout season opened, Longoria wasn't even on the major-league roster. The third baseman had been Tampa Bay's top pick (third overall) in the 2006 draft, and he proved to be a quick study. He climbed swiftly through the farm system and had a huge year in Triple-A in 2007, but he didn't crack the Opening Day lineup in 2008. Then, only 11 games into the season, Rays' third baseman Willy Aybar went down with an injury and Longoria was summoned to take his spot on the hot corner.

The 22-year-old hit the ground running and was red-hot by June. At the break, he had 16 home runs and 53 RBIs and was voted to the All-Star Game by the fans, a rare feat for a rookie. Just as incredibly, the Rays found themselves in first place as the second half of the season began.

The team had built a three-game lead by August 7, when Longoria suffered a broken wrist that threatened to end his

Cinderella season. He missed five weeks, but returned for the stretch drive and powered the Rays with 5 home runs and 14 RBIs over the final 18 games as they fended off the Boston Red Sox to win the AL East. Though he played only 122 games, Longoria finished his freshman campaign with 27 home runs and was the unanimous choice for Rookie of the Year.

The fun was just getting started, though. In Game 1 of the ALDS against the White Sox, Longoria went yard on his first two swings, then added an RBI single in the fifth to pace the Rays to a 6–4 win and eventual victory in the series. All he did in the Championship Series was homer in Games 2 through 5 against the Red Sox, and when the series was pushed to a Game 7, Longoria drove in the tying run with a two-out double. The Rays won the game 3–1 and advanced to their first World Series. The dream ended there, however. After the Rays took Game 1 of the Fall Classic, the Phillies swept the next four. Longoria managed one single in 20 at-bats.

After his incredible debut season, Longoria made a PR blunder: he told the media that he intended to hit 30 home runs and drive in 100 during his sophomore campaign. His coaches and teammates took the 23-year-old to task for the boast, but Longoria backed up his words with his bat. While the Rays posted a mediocre 84–78 record and finished 19 games behind the Yankees, Longoria was outstanding. Not only did he exceed his preseason goals with 33 home runs and 117 RBIs, he took home both the Silver Slugger and Gold Glove Awards, establishing himself as the American League's best third baseman with both the lumber and the leather.

Longoria didn't make any bold predictions before the 2010 season, letting his performance speak for itself. He raised his average to .294, and while he dipped to 22 home runs, he smacked a career-best 46 doubles, and contributed to the Rays' dangerous running game with 15 steals. The club proved that 2008 was no fluke as they again clinched first in the AL East with 96 wins. This time they faced the surprising Texas Rangers in the ALDS, and quickly dropped the first two games at home. When they trailed late in Game 3, just about everyone wrote them off, but the Rays rode a late rally to a win in Game 3 in Arlington. Then Longoria keyed a big win in Game 4 with a pair of doubles and a two-run homer to force a deciding fifth match at Tropicana Field. But the Rangers' Cliff Lee was simply brilliant in that game and promptly ended the Rays' season.

With the wealth of young talent in Tampa Bay, it seems certain that the Rays will continue to be contenders for some time, and Evan Longoria looks to be the new face of a reborn franchise.

$ 24.95
GATE 3
SECTION
FIELD
SEAT
K31
S3KM267
7JUNE11

CAREER HIGHLIGHTS

- set a rookie record with six postseason home runs in 2008
- won two Gold Gloves in his first three seasons at third base (2009–10)
- selected to the AL All-Star Team in each of his first three seasons (2008–10)

3 THIRD BASE

Evan LONGORIA

justin MORNEAU 33

Justin Morneau grew up in New Westminster, British Columbia, and like many other Canadian kids, he played hockey. But he also excelled at basketball and baseball, and it was the latter sport that held out hopes for a pro career. It helped that Justin's dad owned a sporting goods store with a batting cage, where the young athlete honed his left-handed stroke well enough to earn a spot on Canada's World Junior team in 1999, the year he was drafted by Minnesota.

Morneau was in Triple-A to start the 2004 season, but the Twins called him up in May when first baseman Doug Mientkiewicz was injured. His 19 homers in 280 at-bats were enough to convince the team that he was ready for the big time, and Mientkiewicz was traded away. The Twins went on to win their division for the third year in a row, but they bowed out quickly against the Yankees (a postseason result they would later repeat with alarming regularity). Morneau had a couple of doubles in the four-game series, but he batted .235 in his first postseason for the overmatched Twins.

Morneau struggled in 2005, his first full campaign in the majors, and when he began 2006 by hitting .208 in April he was perilously close to returning to Triple-A. By

$ 24.95
GATE 50
SECTION FIELD
SEAT G67
P5TH667
12JULY11

CAREER HIGHLIGHTS

- represented Team Canada at the 2006 and 2009 World Baseball Classics
- two-time winner of the Silver Slugger as the AL's top-hitting first baseman (2006, 2008)
- selected to four AL All-Star Teams (2007–10)

33 FIRST BASE

Justin MORNEAU

June 1 he had improved to .240 with 10 home runs, but this was not the kind of performance the Twins expected from him. Manager Ron Gardenhire laid it all out for his young first baseman, questioning Morneau's maturity and dedication.

Whatever Gardenhire said, it worked. From June 8 to the end of the season, Morneau led the majors with a scorching .362 average. His huge second half allowed him to finish at .321 with 34 homers, 37 doubles, 130 RBIs and a .559 slugging percentage. His hot bat helped the Twins win 96 games and finish atop the AL Central for the fourth time in five years, and Morneau was eager to get a second chance at the postseason. The club met Oakland in the ALDS this time, and he did all he could to key the offense, batting .417 (5-for-12) with two homers, but the Twins scored just seven runs in the three-game sweep. It was some consolation for Morneau that he was voted the league's Most Valuable Player that November.

Morneau set out in 2007 to prove that his MVP season was no fluke. Indeed, during the first four months, he looked like he might even surpass his production of the previous year. By late July he already had 28 home runs, putting him on pace to top 40. But he tanked in the final two months, and from August 1 onward he batted .222 with three homers. His final numbers were still excellent (.271, 31 home runs, 111 RBIs), but the Twins hoped for more consistency.

The six-foot-four first baseman rebounded to hit an even .300 in 2008, and collected 129 RBIs and a franchise record 47 doubles. In his second trip to the All-Star Game, he outslugged Josh Hamilton to win the Home Run Derby, then picked up a pair of hits and scored the winning run in the 15th inning. But he again slumped in the second half, while the Twins and White Sox battled for supremacy in the AL Central. The clubs wound up deadlocked after 162 games, but Minnesota lost the tiebreaker game 1–0.

The club finished in first place in each of the next two seasons, but both times injuries robbed Morneau of a chance to play October baseball. After reaching the 30-homer and 100-RBI plateaus again in 2009, a stress fracture in his back kept him out of the postseason. He was healthy again to start the 2010 campaign and looked forward to clearing the fences in Minnesota's brand new Target Field. Sure enough, he had a sensational first half, and by July 7 he was batting .345 and slugging .618 as the Twins headed to Morneau's native land to face off against the Blue Jays. In the second game of the series, Morneau slid hard into second base on a force play and struck his head against the knee of Toronto infielder John McDonald. It wasn't a particularly dangerous looking play, but Morneau suffered a serious concussion that would keep him sidelined for the rest of the campaign, including the playoffs, where his club was trounced by the Yankees for the second straight year, and the fourth time in the last eight seasons.

The Twins would no doubt agree that if they're ever going to break their streak of early playoff exits, it sure would help to have Morneau in the lineup.

dustin PEDROIA

BOSTON RED SOX ◆ AL East

When Dustin Pedroia showed up at Coors Field for Game 3 of the 2007 World Series, security wouldn't let him in. The guard refused to believe that the diminutive 24-year-old could be a professional ballplayer. Eventually the Red Sox rookie second baseman got in, but Colorado fans wished he hadn't: that afternoon he went 3-for-5 and drove in two runs, as Boston beat the Rockies 10–5 en route to a series' sweep.

Pedroia stands only five-foot-eight and is listed at 165 pounds, but most of that is heart. Playing with the Triple-A Pawtucket Red Sox in 2006, he started slowly before going on a midseason tear that attracted attention in Boston. He was called up in August, and while he hit just .191 in 31 games, one thing quickly became clear: this kid never gave away an at-bat. His swing was hardly a picture of beauty, but in 98 plate appearances he struck out just seven times.

Though he had a mediocre spring training in 2007, Pedroia beat out Alex Cora for the second baseman's job. The Red Sox were probably second-guessing that decision after Pedroia's terrible first month, but as May opened, the feisty infielder hit his stride, taking his average from .172 to .336 by June 3, a stretch that included a 14-game hitting streak. He continued swinging a hot bat in August and September (.324 over those two months) when the Red Sox were fending off the Yankees to capture the AL East title.

The rookie then chipped in with 10 hits in the ALCS against Cleveland, and the Red Sox won Games 5, 6 and 7 in blowouts to advance to the World Series. Boston was pitted against Colorado, who looked like the team of destiny. The Rockies entered the Fall Classic having won an astonishing 21 of their past 22 games, including sweeps of both the Phillies and the Diamondbacks in the NL playoffs.

Boston was the host in Game 1, and the first batter the Rockies faced was Pedroia. He took the first pitch

for a strike. Then he hit the next one over the Green Monster to begin what turned into a 13–1 rout. The Red Sox never let up, and they disposed of Colorado in four straight to take their second World Series in four years. Pedroia took home the AL Rookie of the Year award to go along with his championship ring.

The second baseman followed up his brilliant freshman year with a more consistent season in 2008. When he got hot he was relentless, and he strung together hitting streaks of 14, 17 and 10 games. The hits kept piling up, and by the end of the season he was tied with Ichiro Suzuki for tops in the majors (213), led the loop with 54 doubles and 118 runs scored, and showed surprising power with 17 home runs. His .326 average, a record for Red Sox second sackers, fell two points shy of the batting title.

After the season, Pedroia snagged both the Silver Slugger and the Gold Glove. He had committed just six errors in 733 chances for a .992 fielding percentage. Red Sox fans then waited to see whether their second baseman's performance would be enough to snag the game's highest individual honor. It was: Pedroia edged out Justin Morneau in the voting for the Most Valuable Player award.

Pedroia's average fell to .296 in 2009, but he still led the AL with 115 runs scored and was third in the league with 48 doubles, to go along with 15 homers and 20 steals. Pitchers were finding it more and more difficult to throw a strike past him: over his career, his strikeout rate is less than 7.5 percent, a remarkably low figure that puts him in the same conversation with another great Red Sox infielder, Hall of Famer Wade Boggs.

In June of 2010, the Red Sox returned to Coors Field for an interleague series, setting up a rematch of the 2007 Fall Classic. Again, security regretted letting him past the gate. In the third match, Pedroia went 5-for-5 with three home runs, the last of which won the game in the 10th inning. But the next day, he fouled a pitch off his left foot, sustaining a fracture that would ultimately end his season. It also gave pitchers a temporary reprieve from one of the toughest outs in the game.

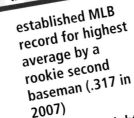

$ 24.95

GATE 31

SECTION FIELD

SEAT A21

G9SS568

6JUNE11

CAREER HIGHLIGHTS

- established MLB record for highest average by a rookie second baseman (.317 in 2007)
- one of only eight players to have won Rookie of the Year, MVP, a Gold Glove and a World Series
- named to the AL All-Star Team three times (2008–10)

15 SECOND BASE

Dustin PEDROIA

albert PUJOLS

5

Many great hitters take time to reach their prime, but Albert Pujols arrived in the big leagues as a fully formed superstar. With the possible exceptions of Ted Williams and Joe DiMaggio, there simply has never been a player whose first decade in the majors was so consistently magnificent. Pujols is the only player ever to bat .300 or better with at least 30 home runs and 100 RBIs in each of his first 10 seasons, and the only one to hit 400 home runs in that span.

The ascendance of Albert Pujols is all the more remarkable when you consider that no one expected it. As a teenager he was a bit heavy, ungainly, and didn't excel at any defensive position. When the Cardinals drafted him in 1999, he went 402nd overall. He played one year in the minors and landed a job with the Cardinals in 2001 only because left fielder Bobby Bonilla was injured. But the 21-year-old shocked everyone by batting .351 with 16 home runs in April and May. Determined to get his bat into the lineup every day, the Cards played him in left field, right field, third base and first base, making him the first player ever to start at least 30 games at four different positions in one season. He wound up leading the team in almost every offensive category as he finished at .329 with 37 homers, 47 doubles, 130 RBIs and 112 runs scored — unbelievable numbers for a rookie.

In his sophomore season, Pujols posted similar numbers to those of his debut and finished a distant second to Barry Bonds in the MVP voting. Then he led the majors with a .359 average in 2003, to go along with 43 homers, 51 doubles, 137 runs scored and a dizzying OPS of 1.106. When the Cardinals won the NL pennant in 2004, Pujols slugged 46 home runs and led the league in extra-base hits (99) and total bases (389). He also had his best postseason to date, batting .414, including 14-for-28 with four home runs to take MVP honors in the NL Championship Series against Houston.

CAREER HIGHLIGHTS

- leads all active players in batting average (.331), on-base percentage (.426) and slugging (.624)
- from 2001 through 2010, leads all NL players in every Triple Crown category: .331 average, 408 home runs, and 1,230 RBIs
- three-time NL MVP (2005, 2008, 2009)

5 FIRST BASE

Albert **PUJOLS**

The first baseman finally won his first MVP award in 2005, when he led the majors in runs scored for the third straight year, the first person to accomplish that since Pete Rose. Facing the Astros in the NLCS again that year, Pujols came up in the ninth inning of Game 5 with the Cards trailing 4–2 and facing elimination. With two on and two out, he crushed an 0–1 pitch from Brad Lidge way over the left-field wall for a game-winning three-run homer. The exultant Redbirds lost the next day, however, and the dream would have to wait another year.

Pujols opened 2006 by hitting 14 home runs in April, and he would certainly have finished the season with more than 50 had he not missed most of June with a muscle strain. As it was, he belted a career-high 49 and just missed accomplishing the extraordinary feat of tallying more homers than strikeouts, as he whiffed just 50 times. After a solid performance in the first two postseason series that October, Pujols hit just .200 in the Fall Classic, but the underdog Cards shocked everyone by knocking off the Detroit Tigers in five games.

When Pujols put together back-to-back MVP seasons in 2008 and 2009, he did so with Triple Crown–type numbers. He batted a lofty .357 in the first of those campaigns, then led the majors with 47 dingers the following year. He also topped all hitters in slugging, OPS and total bases both seasons. Amazingly, he accomplished all of this with a damaged right elbow that required surgery to reposition the ulnar nerve in October 2008, and again to remove bone spurs after the 2009 season. He was the runner-up to Joey Votto in the MVP voting in 2010, when he led the NL with 42 home runs, 118 RBIs and 115 runs scored, and he picked up his second Gold Glove and sixth Silver Slugger Award for first basemen. He suffered from painful tendinitis in the left elbow during the last two months, but missed only three games all season.

A deeply religious man, baseball's finest player works tirelessly with his Pujols Family Foundation supporting children and adults with Down Syndrome, and he regularly arranges for medical care to be delivered to the poor in the Dominican Republic, his native country. For Albert Pujols, being a great ballplayer means first becoming a great human being and then playing naturally.

hanley
RAMIREZ

2

When Hanley Ramirez signed with Boston in the summer of 2000, the 16-year-old shortstop hoped to someday anchor the Red Sox infield behind his fellow countryman and hero, Pedro Martinez. As it turned out, Ramirez got just two at bats with the Red Sox — striking out both times — before the club dealt him to Florida after the 2005 season.

The trade worked out well for the Red Sox. They acquired Josh Beckett and Mike Lowell, who led Boston to a World Series title in 2007, a year when the Marlins finished dead last in the NL East. But down in Miami, Hanley Ramirez has become perhaps the game's best young player, and the centerpiece of a Marlins franchise that is looking to regain its past glory.

After an impressive spring training, Ramirez was the Marlins' Opening Day shortstop and leadoff man in 2006. He made an immediate impact, hitting safely in his first eight games and posting a .379 OBP and seven stolen bases in April. And while he slumped badly in June and much of July, he finished with a bang. In September alone, he swatted 43 hits, including 21 for extra bases, and when the season was over, Ramirez topped all National League rookies in batting average (.292), hits (185), doubles (46), runs (119) and stolen bases (51). His hot streak in the final month helped secure Ramirez NL Rookie of the Year honors.

It's rare for a first-year phenom to follow up with an even better sophomore season, but Ramirez did exactly that in

2007. Despite playing the second half with nagging pain from a partially dislocated shoulder he suffered in July, Ramirez challenged for the batting title, finishing at .332. His 212 hits included 29 homers and 48 doubles, and his 359 total bases were third-best in the league.

Despite his high OBP and back-to-back seasons with 50-plus steals, it was clear that the leadoff position was a waste of Ramirez's power. In early 2008, the Marlins experimented with him batting third in the lineup, and the following year he settled in at the three-spot. Ramirez flourished in that role, winning his first batting title in 2009 with a .342 average. He also batted .373 with runners in scoring position, which helped

him collect 106 RBIs. He led the Marlins to an 87–75 season, good enough for second in the NL East, and their best record since their World Series championship in 2003.

The Marlins and their star struggled in 2010. Ramirez had been criticized for not hustling in the past, but the breaking point came in a game against Arizona in mid-May. While trying to field a popup over his head, Ramirez inadvertently kicked the ball into left field and then slowly jogged after it while two Diamondbacks raced around to score. A furious manager Fredi Gonzalez took Ramirez out of the game and benched him the following day as well. The manager and his marquee player had sparred many times before, but it soon became clear where the Marlins organization was pinning its future hopes: Gonzalez was fired a month later. Ramirez, meanwhile, was voted to the All-Star Game as the NL's starting shortstop for the third time, and even finished second in the Home Run Derby.

Many of Han-Ram's final 2010 numbers (.300 average, .475 slugging percentage) were well off his previous highs, and the Marlins slipped below .500. But with a promising young pitching staff and baseball's most dangerous combination of power and speed, Florida should be a perennial contender in the tough NL East.

CAREER HIGHLIGHTS

- first NL rookie to collect more than 110 runs and 50 stolen bases (2006)

- was one home run shy of becoming the third player in MLB history with 30 homers and 50 stolen bases in the same season (2007)

- voted starting shortstop on the NL All-Star Team 2008–10

2 SHORTSTOP

Hanley RAMIREZ

brian
ROBERTS

BALTIMORE ORIOLES ◆ AL East

Brian Roberts couldn't attract much attention from the scouts in high school. At a wispy five-foot-nine, he was hardly an imposing figure at the plate, though he could certainly fly around the bases and play a slick shortstop. When no one selected him in the MLB draft and no colleges waved any tempting offers in front of him, Roberts enrolled at the University of North Carolina at Chapel Hill, where his dad coached the baseball team. At least there he'd have an opportunity to play.

To everyone's shock, the diminutive infielder turned out to be the team's best hitter. He batted .427 and stole 47 bases on his way to being named NCAA Freshman of the Year. By his junior year, *Baseball America* named him the top defensive player in the nation, and Roberts finally attracted the attention of major-league bird dogs. Baltimore grabbed the 21-year-old in the 1999 draft, and

two years later he was playing alongside future Hall of Famer Cal Ripken, who was in his final season with the Orioles in 2001.

Roberts worked hard to secure a regular job as the O's second baseman and leadoff man, and the switch-hitting speedster made his mark with a league-best 50 doubles and 29 steals in 2004. The next season, the perennially weak Orioles flirted with respectability: they opened the campaign 31–20 and were in first place as late as June 23. A lot of that was thanks to Roberts, who batted .368 in April and May, including a 20-game hit streak.

The Orioles collapsed in July and eventually finished 21 games off the lead. But it was a breakout season for Roberts. He socked 11 home runs in the first two months — one shy of the number he'd hit in

the previous four seasons. Although his teammates included Rafael Palmeiro and Sammy Sosa, it was the 175-pound Roberts who suddenly found himself facing allegations of using steroids. (He later stated that he had done so only once, and it was in 2003.) By September, he was enjoying a .314 average and had raised his slugging percentage from .376 the previous year to .515. Everything almost came to crashing halt, though, when he suffered a career-threatening injury in late September. In a collision at first base, Roberts dislocated his left elbow and tore a tendon and a ligament. He had successful surgery ten days later, however, and was ready for Opening Day the next season.

Baltimore's woes continued in 2007, when they lost 93 games, including the most lopsided game in MLB history — a 30–3 drubbing at the hands of the Texas Rangers. (Roberts was 3-for-5 in the match.) Their second sacker was one of the few bright spots that year: Roberts led the American League with 50 steals and was selected to his second All-Star Team.

Before the 2008 season, the O's dealt away Miguel Tejada and Erik Bedard in an attempt to rebuild the team with younger talent. With Roberts now 30 years old and his contract about to expire, his name came

up in trade rumors constantly. He didn't let the gossip affect his play, however. He reached the 50-double mark again and slugged .450, his best mark in three years. Still holding down the role of leadoff man, he swiped 40 bases and matched his career high with 107 runs scored.

In the winter of 2009, Roberts inked a four-year contract extension that will keep him in black and orange until 2013. Then, at age 31, he went on to have one of his most productive seasons ever. He amassed 56 two-baggers to go along with 16 home runs, and established new personal bests with 110 runs scored and 79 RBIs, a remarkable number for a leadoff hitter.

Four games into the 2010 campaign, Roberts strained an abdominal muscle sliding into second, and the injury forced him to miss 92 games. In the meantime, the Orioles set about burying themselves deep in the AL East cellar, with an appalling 25–59 record in the first half. Roberts returned on July 23, and a week later the Orioles replaced manager Dave Tremblay with Buck Showalter. The result was a completely different team. The O's went 34–23 the rest of the way, the best mark in the American League, offering hope that Roberts and the Orioles can look forward to a more prosperous decade than the one that just ended.

TICKET

$ 24.95
GATE **34**
SECTION **CLUB**
SEAT **F14**
R4SD887
18SEPT11

CAREER HIGHLIGHTS

- only switch-hitter ever to collect 45 doubles, 15 home runs and 20 steals in a season (2005 and 2009)
- set AL record for doubles in a season by a switch hitter with 56 (2009)
- selected to the AL All-Star Team in 2005 and 2007

1   SECOND BASE

Brian ROBERTS

alex RODRIGUEZ

13

NEW YORK YANKEES ◆ AL East

Alex Rodriguez's list of achievements is dizzying: three MVP awards, five AL home run titles, 13 All-Star selections, 10 Silver Sluggers and a record 13 straight seasons with at least 30 home runs and 100 RBIs. There is no doubt that he is one of the greatest players of all time.

Rodriguez debuted with the Seattle Mariners when he was still only 18. The boy wonder played his first full season in 1996 at age 20, and he had a year like no one had ever seen from a middle infielder at the start of his career. He won the batting title with a .358 average and socked 36 home runs. His 141 runs, 91 extra-base hits and .631 slugging percentage were all records for shortstops.

Rodriguez passed the 40-homer plateau each season from 1998 to 2000, and in the first of those years he added 46 steals to become the third 40–40 player in history. With five years of major-league service under his belt, he tested the free agent market in the winter of 2001 and signed with the Texas Rangers for a staggering $252 million over 10 years.

A-Rod was simply fantastic during his three years in Arlington, posting seasons of 52, 57 and 47 home runs. He won two Gold Gloves and his first MVP award. But despite his heroics, the Rangers finished at least 25 games back each year, and Rodriguez wanted out of Texas. The Yankees agreed to send Alfonso Soriano to the Rangers if Texas would continue to cover part of A-Rod's gargantuan paycheck.

The newest Yankee quickly learned how things worked in New York. It didn't matter that Rodriguez (now playing third base) hit 36 home runs during his first year in pinstripes, or that he followed that up in 2005 with his second MVP Award. What mattered was that he went 2-for-17 in the final four games of the 2004 ALCS against the arch-rival Red Sox, allowing Boston to storm back from a three-game deficit. Over the following two postseasons he was 3-for-29 (.103).

Rodriguez had a career year in 2007, even by his own

lofty standards. He reached the 50-homer plateau for the third time, set personal bests with 156 RBIs and a .645 slugging percentage, and he was an easy choice for his third MVP Award. His playoff story was the same, though. He went hitless with men on base during the ALDS, and the Yankees bowed out to Cleveland in four games.

In the offseason, Rodriguez shocked the baseball world when he announced he would not exercise his option to rejoin the Yankees in 2008. A few weeks later, though, he changed his mind and inked a 10-year, $275-million dollar deal. He did, after all, still have some unfinished business in New York. He did his part in 2008, leading the league with a .573 slugging percentage, and despite a stint on the DL he became the first player in history to collect 35 home runs, 100 RBIs and 100 runs in 11 straight seasons. But the Yankees finished third in 2008, ending a string of 13 consecutive trips to the playoffs.

2009 was an eventful year for Alex Rodriguez. In February, he admitted that he had used performance-enhancing drugs during his three seasons with the Rangers. Then he needed surgery for a hip injury and missed the first month of the season. From the day he returned, however, New York went 90–44 as they ran away with the AL East and gave Rodriguez his fifth playoff opportunity as a Yankee.

This time A-Rod was a wrecking crew. He led the club in postseason batting average (.365), runs scored (15), and home runs (6), and his 18 RBIs were one short of the all-time record. Most important, he came through in the clutch over and over. He tied Game 2 of the ALDS against Minnesota with a two-run jack in the bottom of the ninth, and socked another game-tying home run in the 11th against the Angels in Game 2 of the Championship Series. When the Yanks were down 3–0 to the Phillies in Game 3 of the World Series, Rodriguez hit a two-run blast that turned the tide, and New York went on to win 8–5. Then he broke a 4–4 tie with an RBI double with two outs in the ninth in Game 4. When the Yankees took the series in six games, A-Rod finally had a World Series ring in his eighth trip to the postseason.

Rodriguez spent more time on the DL in 2010, but he still reached 30 homers and drove in 125 runs in only 137 games. During the season he passed Frank Robinson, Mark McGwire and Sammy Sosa to move into sixth on the all-time home run list with 613, and he needs 467 RBIs to surpass Hank Aaron's career mark of 2,297. If he can stay healthy until he's 40, Alex Rodriguez will take a run at some of the most hallowed records in baseball.

$ 24.95

GATE 2
SECTION
CLUB
SEAT
AS26
S5EB675
15JULY11

CAREER HIGHLIGHTS

- leads all players in home runs (424) and RBI (1,236) over the last decade (2001–10)

- owns MLB single-season records for home runs by a shortstop (57 in 2002) and by a third baseman (54 in 2007)

- youngest player to reach 600 career home runs (35 years, 8 days old)

13 THIRD BASE

Alex RODRIGUEZ

mark
TEIXEIRA

25

NEW YORK YANKEES ◆ AL East

Growing up in Annapolis, Maryland, Mark Teixeira went to a lot of Baltimore Orioles games, but he usually wore a Yankees cap. His favorite player was Don Mattingly, the sweet-swinging Yankees first baseman, and when he made it to the big leagues, he even wore Mattingly's number 23 on his Texas Rangers jersey. So when Teixeira entertained offers as a free agent after the 2008 season, his decision to become the Yankees' first baseman was a no-brainer.

The teenaged Teixeira was one of the hottest high-school players in the U.S., and the Boston Red Sox were courting him as the 1998 draft approached. The Bosox had led him to believe they were going to select him early, and when they waited until the ninth round Teixeira felt snubbed and chose not to sign. Instead, he enrolled at Georgia Tech, where the switch hitter had an outstanding college career, batting .409 with 36 homers and 165 RBIs over three seasons. When he was eligible for the draft again in 2001, Teixeira went in the first round, chosen fifth overall by the Rangers.

Teixeira had a fine rookie season with Texas in 2003, leading all major-league freshmen with 26 home runs and 60 extra-base hits. The following year he pounded 38 homers and tallied 112 RBIs and 101 runs to win a Silver Slugger in just his second season. On August 17, 2004, Teixeira struck out his first time up, and then doubled, homered, tripled and singled in his next four at-bats to become just the second Ranger to hit for the cycle.

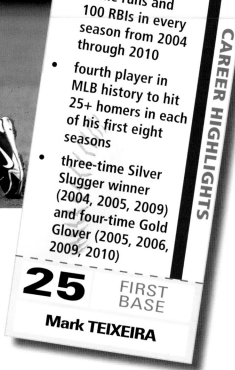

$ 24.95
GATE 51
SECTION CLUB
SEAT L6
K5SR185
4AUG11

CAREER HIGHLIGHTS

• one of only three players with 30+ home runs and 100 RBIs in every season from 2004 through 2010

• fourth player in MLB history to hit 25+ homers in each of his first eight seasons

• three-time Silver Slugger winner (2004, 2005, 2009) and four-time Gold Glover (2005, 2006, 2009, 2010)

25   FIRST BASE

Mark TEIXEIRA

Only two other switch hitters in MLB history have accomplished the feat with a pair of hits from each side of the plate.

Teixeira put together an MVP-type season in 2005. Playing on a powerful Rangers club that led the American League in long balls, he swatted 43 homers, drove in 144 runs (a record for switch hitters), topped the league in total bases, and capped it all with a .301 average. He also led AL first basemen in total chances while making only three errors for a fielding percentage of .998. While Teixeira did not win the league's top award that fall, he copped his second straight Silver Slugger and his first Gold Glove.

Just before the trading deadline in July 2007, Teixeira was part of the season's biggest swap. The Rangers dealt him to the Atlanta Braves, returning him to the state where he had excelled during his college years. Teixeira had quite a homecoming: in August he batted .315 with a .640 slugging percentage, notching 10 homers and 32 RBIs to win the National League's Player of the Month.

Knowing he would be a free agent at the end of the campaign, the Braves sent Teixeira to the Los Angeles Angels of Anaheim in late July 2008. The Halos already had a huge lead in the AL West, and Teixeira got his first taste of the postseason that year. In four games against the Red Sox in the ALDS, he was 7-for-15 (.467), but the Angels lost the series in four close games.

After bouncing among three teams in 12 months, Teixeira was anxious to settle down, and he inked an eight-year deal with the Yankees early in 2009. A notoriously slow starter, he was still batting under .200 six weeks into his first season in pinstripes. Then he slugged 13 home runs in May and stayed hot all through the second half, hitting .313 with 18 long balls after the break. He wound up tied for the AL lead in home runs with 39, as well as a league-high 122 RBIs. The Yankees won 103 games and cruised through the Twins, Angels and Phillies to win their first World Series since 2000. Teixeira batted a lowly .180 in 15 postseason matches, but he did make an impact. In Game 2 of the ALDS against Minnesota, with the Yankees down 3–1 in the ninth, Teixeira singled and scored on Alex Rodriguez's game-tying homer, and then won it in the 11th with a walk-off blast.

Teixeira's 2010 season was bookended with poor months (.136 in April, .220 in September), and his .256 average was the lowest of his career. But he still led the American League with a career-high 113 runs scored (it helped to have A-Rod and Robinson Cano batting behind him) and he picked up his fourth Gold Glove. Teixeira also continued his string of seven seasons with at least 30 homers and 100 RBIs, becoming the third Yankee first baseman to reach those benchmarks more than once. The other two? Hall of Famer Lou Gehrig and a guy named Don Mattingly.

troy TULOWITZKI

2

When the Colorado Rockies played host to the Yankees in an interleague series in June 2007, Troy Tulowitzki sought out his hero in the visitors' clubhouse. The freshman shortstop wanted to talk with Derek Jeter, who offered the 22-year-old some friendly encouragement and gave him an autographed bat. Three months later, Tulowitzki was doing just what Jeter did in 1996: showing remarkable leadership as a rookie and leading his club to the World Series.

A two-time All-American at Long Beach State, Troy Tulowitzki was drafted seventh overall by the Rockies in 2005, and a mere 15 months later earned the full-time shortstop's job in Colorado. Tulowitzki started making history almost immediately. On April 29, 2007, the 46th game of his MLB career, he snagged a line drive off the bat of Atlanta's Chipper Jones and completed an unassisted triple play — just the 13th in history. He showcased his sure hands and tremendous throwing arm all season long, leading MLB shortstops in fielding percentage, total chances, putouts, assists and double plays.

Tulo was slower to warm up with the bat. He batted .244 in April and was homerless in 121 plate appearances during May. By the end of that month, the Rockies were 25–29 and 6½ games back in the NL West. They couldn't make up any ground over the next three months, but then they staged an extraordinary September rally, winning 14 of their final 15 games. Tulowitzki knocked 15 homers and drove in 61 runs in the second half, many of them in clutch situations. When the Rockies forced a one-game playoff with the Padres to determine the wild card winner, Tulo had four hits (three for extra bases) and three runs. He smacked an RBI double in the 13th and then scored the equalizer as Colorado rallied to win. Overall in his amazing first season, Tulowitzki batted .291, slugged 24 homers, scored 104 runs and drove in 99. He looked more like a rookie in the postseason, however: clearly overmatched, he went 8-for-41 (.195) and struck out 15 times.

CAREER HIGHLIGHTS

- set NL record for home runs (24) and MLB mark for RBIs (99) by a rookie shortstop (2007)

- owns a career .985 fielding percentage and led NL shortstops in 2007 and 2010

- selected to the NL All-Star Team in 2010

2 SHORTSTOP

Troy TULOWITZKI

Two stints on the disabled list held Tulowitzki to 101 games in his sophomore season, but his struggles weren't just physical. He felt enormous pressure to repeat his brilliant 2007 performance, and whenever he had a bad game, he was furious with himself. He was batting .152 when he tore a quadriceps muscle in April, and then suffered a foolish self-inflicted injury that might have been much worse: with his average down to .166 on July 4, he got frustrated after being removed from a game and smashed his bat into the ground; it shattered, embedding shards of maple into his right palm. He needed 16 stitches and was fortunate that he didn't permanently damage his throwing hand. But he learned his lesson: in his first game back, he went 5-for-5 and batted .327 during the remainder of the season.

Tulowitzki put his bat to more productive use in 2009, when he led his club with 32 home runs, 92 RBIs, 101 runs scored, and 300 total bases. He even swiped 20 bags to become the first 20–20 infielder in Rockies' history. Tulo again showed himself to be a clutch performer by posting a .344 average in the second half as the Rockies challenged for a postseason berth. On August 10, he hit for the cycle and drove in seven runs in an 11–5 win over the Cubs. And during the 18-game stretch ending October 2, he batted .435 and went yard eight times as the Rockies nailed down the wild card.

The pattern of explosive finishes continued for Tulowitzki in 2010. He was batting .306 when he broke his wrist in mid-June and missed a month, and he had just 12 home runs by the end of August. Then Tulo went on a tear that surpassed anything he'd done to date. During a 15-game span starting September 3 he blasted 14 home runs, and he went on to collect a staggering 40 RBIs in that final month. (The only player to have more homers and RBIs in September was Babe Ruth in 1927.) Tulowitzki's amazing month included a seven-RBI game against the Dodgers, and a five-RBI performance 10 days later that included a walk-off 10th-inning double against the Giants' lights-out closer Brian Wilson.

Tulowitzki captured his first Silver Slugger in 2010 with a career-best .315 average and .568 slugging percentage, to go along with 27 homers and 95 RBIs. He also snagged an overdue Gold Glove, finally earning recognition for his stellar defensive play. In November, the Rockies offered him a $158-million contract extension that's good until 2020, when he'll be 35 years old. The deal brought Troy Tulowitzki one step closer to becoming a franchise player in the mold of Derek Jeter and Cal Ripken. There's no question he has their talent: the only question is whether he'll match their longevity.

chase
UTLEY

26

Not many second basemen can pound 25 or 30 home runs and collect 100 RBIs in the heart of a batting order. Ryne Sandberg and Joe Morgan did it, and they ended up in the Hall of Fame. Jeff Kent did it in his prime as well, and he's a likely candidate for Cooperstown, too. Chase Utley is a long way from having a plaque etched with his name, but his performance since 2005 is on par with those elite second-sackers.

Born in Pasadena, California, Utley accepted a baseball scholarship from UCLA, where he batted .342 with 174 RBIs over three seasons. In his junior year, he was named Outstanding Player of the NCAA Regionals and got noticed by the Philadelphia Phillies, who took him in the first round of the 2001 draft. Utley made his debut in April 2003, and his first major-league hit was a grand slam in a 9–1 win over the Rockies. The party didn't last, however, and Utley was back in the minors by May, and he spent the rest of that season and all of 2004 bouncing between the farm and the big club.

In 2005, the Phils decided to platoon Utley and Placido Polanco at second base, but by early June it was clear who the future belonged to: Polanco was shipped to Detroit and Utley assumed the everyday role. That move looked pretty good at the end of the season when Utley had compiled a .291 average, a .540 slugging percentage, 39 doubles and 28 homers. He also drove in 105 runs to set a Philly record for second basemen.

Utley put together an outstanding season in 2006. He batted .309 with 32 home runs, 40 doubles, 102 RBIs, and a league-leading 131 runs scored. From June 23 to August 3, he compiled a 35-game hit streak, tied for the tenth-longest in major-league history. He may have had a shot at the MVP award in 2007 had he not missed a month with an injury. He was hitting .336 with 17 homers and 82 RBIs on July 26 when he had his right hand broken by a pitch. (Utley has the dubious honor of leading the majors in HBPs every year from

2007 through 2009.) Despite undergoing surgery and having a metal pin inserted, he returned earlier than expected and went 3-for-5 with a home run in his first game back. He finished the year with a robust .332 average, third best in the league.

The Phillies had been swept in the first round of the 2007 postseason and were looking to redeem themselves the following year. Utley set the tone with 11 homers in April and eight more in May. (Twice that season he homered in five straight games.) He finished the year at .292 with 33 home runs and 104 RBIs as the Phillies won their second NL East title. Although Utley hit just .220 in the postseason, he made one of the best defensive plays of the year in Game 5 of the World Series. With the score tied 3–3 in the seventh, the Tampa Bay Rays had Jason Bartlett on second with two out when Akinori Iwamura grounded one up the middle. Utley backhanded the ball deep in the hole and had no play at first, but he faked a throw in that direction, tricking Bartlett into making a dash for home. Utley then fired an off-balance throw to his catcher, who nailed Bartlett to end the inning and preserve the tie. The Phillies scored in the bottom of the inning and won 4–3 to clinch their first championship since 1980.

Utley needed hip surgery in the offseason and team doctors suggested it might be June before he would be able to return. But the second baseman was in the lineup on opening day, batted .342 with seven homers in April, and that season he swiped a career-high 23 bases without being caught. The Phillies got to the Fall Classic again in 2009, and Utley belted two solo home runs off Yankee ace CC Sabathia in Game 1, which Philadelphia won 6–1. Utley homered again in Game 4, and went yard twice in Game 5 to tie Reggie Jackson's record of five home runs in a World Series. This was the Yankees' year, however, and the Phillies lost in six games.

Early in his career, Utley was a question mark in the infield, and he hasn't been able to shake that label despite dramatic improvements in his defense. He's never won a Gold Glove — an award based almost entirely on reputation — but statistical analysts handed him a Fielding Bible Award in 2010 as the best defensive second baseman in the game based on the number of runs he saved with his glove and his arm.

$ 24.95
GATE 16
SECTION FIELD
SEAT S60
E8VC128
1SEPT08

CAREER HIGHLIGHTS

- one of only three second baseman in MLB history to have four straight 100-RBI seasons (2005–08)
- four-time Silver Slugger Award winner (2006–09)
- five-time NL All-Star (2006–10)

26 SECOND BASE

Chase UTLEY

joey VOTTO

CINCINNATI REDS ◆ NL Central

Unlike most athletic kids who grow up in Toronto, Joey Votto had little interest in hockey. He and his dad were rabid baseball fans who played catch with each other whenever they could. One of their fondest memories came when Joey was 10 and they watched Joe Carter belt a walk-off homer to win the 1993 World Series for the Blue Jays.

When Votto was in high school he set his sights squarely on a career in baseball. He even swung a wood bat, figuring that's what he'd have to use when he eventually made it to the big time. For his final high-school at-bat, however, his teammates egged him until he agreed to step to the plate with a stick of shiny aluminum. He promptly blasted a tape-measure home run that his coach described as "without question the farthest ball I've ever seen hit in high school."

However, Votto was no overnight success. After being drafted by the Cincinnati Reds in 2002, he spent six full seasons in the minors. Finally in 2007, having worked his way up to Triple-A, he belted 22 long balls and drove in 92 runs, and the Reds decided to make him a September call-up. He responded with a .321 average and a .548

slugging percentage (thanks to four home runs and seven doubles) in his one month of action.

As Opening Day dawned in 2008, the Reds were coming off a 72–90 season with no reason to expect much improvement. Still, manager Dusty Baker wasn't convinced that Votto was ready for the everyday job, so he used him both at first base and as a pinch hitter. By early May, however, Votto was slugging over .500 and there was no longer any reason to platoon him.

Then, in August, tragedy struck. Votto's father, whose dream was to see his son play in the majors, died suddenly at 52 years old. The young slugger missed six games to be with his family, but then he bottled up his grief and played out the rest of the season. He channelled his emotions into his play, and his performance was better than it had ever been. He batted .341 with 11 homers over the final two months and wound up leading National League freshmen in most offensive categories, including batting average (.297), homers (24) and slugging (.506). Despite these numbers, however, the NL Rookie of the Year award went to Cubs' catcher Geovany Soto.

Votto opened the 2009 campaign even stronger than he'd ended the previous one, and by late May his average was above .370. But there were clues that something was wrong. Three times that month he removed himself from games, despite having no obvious injury. Votto later revealed that for months he had been quietly suffering from terrible bouts of depression and anxiety stemming from his father's death. Finally, on May 30, he took a month-long break from baseball to seek counselling.

When he returned, he picked up right where he'd left off. While the Reds endured their ninth straight losing season, Votto's final numbers were outstanding. He batted .322, slugged .567 and collected 25 home runs and 84 RBIs despite his abbreviated campaign.

Few forecasters expected the Reds to be a powerhouse in 2010, but the team did look much

$ 24.95

GATE 23

SECTION CLUB

SEAT H12

S5SR185

2SEPT11

CAREER HIGHLIGHTS

- established a franchise record for RBIs by a rookie with 84 (2008)
- Voted NL MVP in 2010
- voted to the NL All-Star Team in 2010

19   FIRST BASE

Joey VOTTO

improved with a rejuvenated Scott Rolen at third, young talent like Jay Bruce and Drew Stubbs in the outfield, and Johnny Cueto on the mound. As it turned out, when the All-Star break rolled around, the Reds were 49–41, one game ahead of the pack in the NL Central. Votto was leading the way with a tremendous first half, including a .314 average, 22 homers and 60 RBIs.

The Reds played consistent baseball the rest of the way and locked up their first division title since 1995. The postseason was not so kind, however. The Phillies' Roy Halladay no-hit them in the opener of the NLDS, and the Reds meekly dropped the next two games and made a quick exit. Votto managed one single in 10 at-bats.

However, the first baseman's regular-season line included a .324 average, 37 homers, 113 RBIs, 106 runs scored, and the highest OBP (.424) and slugging percentage (.600) in the majors. That added up to 31 of 32 first-place votes for the National League's Most Valuable Player Award.

Votto's performance on the field since 2008 has been remarkable, given the personal issues he's dealt with. Moreover, his willingness to go public about his emotional battles has helped fans see the human side of professional athletes.

david WRIGHT

NEW YORK METS ◆ NL East

Shortly after David Wright debuted with the Mets in 2004, the cover of the *New York Post's* sports section featured a photo of the 21-year-old third baseman under the headline "Great Wright Hope." At the time, the Mets were in the middle of their third consecutive losing season. Wright's quick evolution from prospect to proven hitter was a major factor in the turnaround that saw the team win the National League East division title in 2006 and contend for the wild card in the next two seasons.

Wright began his 2004 campaign in Double-A, where he batted .363 with 10 homers in 60 games. On July 21, the Mets called him up when Ty Wigginton was injured, and that was that. He manned third base in every game for the rest of that year and has been a fixture at the hot corner ever since. In 263 at-bats that first year, Wright led NL freshmen with a .293 average and slugged .525 with 14 home runs. Not bad for a kid who had been given no chance of making the team in spring training.

The Mets had high hopes for 2005. They signed free agents Pedro Martinez and Carlos Beltran in the offseason, and the team's other hot prospect, Jose Reyes, was slated to be the everyday shortstop. But it was Wright who turned out to be the dominant offensive player in the lineup. Showing that his rookie numbers were no fluke, he led the club with a .306 average, 42 doubles, 102 RBIs and an OPS of .912. He hit 27 home runs, 11 more than Beltran, whose salary was 36 times higher.

Wright began the 2006 season with a huge first half. After slugging .585 in April, he had three walk-off RBIs in May, and by the break he had amassed 20 homers and a franchise-record 74 RBIs. That earned him a trip to his first All-Star Game, where he finished second in the Home Run Derby to the hulking Ryan Howard. Not to be denied his own long-ball glory, Wright attacked a Kenny Rogers changeup in his first

All-Star at-bat and launched it over the left field wall to knot the score at 1–1. After that impressive showing, Wright's power abandoned him in the second half of 2006. He was homerless from July 29 to August 29, and again from September 1 to 22. The Mets won the division and swept the Dodgers in the NLDS before being eliminated by the Cardinals, with Wright batting a disappointing .216 in his first postseason.

Mets fans worried when Wright opened 2007 by batting .244 without a single home run. However, he turned everything around by socking eight homers in May and six more in June, erasing any doubts about whether he really was a power hitter. Wright also surprised fans — and opposing pitchers and catchers — with his ability to steal, despite only average speed. On August 30 he swiped his 30th bag of the year, and on September 16 he hit his 30th home run, becoming the third Met to join the 30–30 club, and one of only five players to accomplish the feat before age 25. His 330 total bases that year were a franchise record, and he picked up the Silver Slugger and his first Gold Glove at third base.

The Mets imploded at the end of 2007, blowing a seven-game lead with only 17 left to play, and they missed the postseason again in 2008, despite occupying first place as late as September 19. Wright, however, had perhaps his best season to date: he batted .302 with a career-high 33 homers and 124 RBIs, good for second in the National League. He also smacked 42 doubles to become only the second player in MLB history to collect at least 40 doubles and 25 home runs in four straight seasons.

Wright was on his way to batting over .300 for the fifth year in a row in 2009 when he had the scariest moment of his career. In mid-August, the Giants' Matt Cain hit him square on the temple with a fastball, and Wright missed two weeks with a concussion. When he returned on September 1, Wright showed no signs of ill health, and he drove in 17 runs in the final month, including six in a 10–9 win over the Phillies.

Wright's average slipped to .283 in 2010, the lowest mark of his career, but his power returned. After hitting just 10 homers the year before, Wright went yard 29 times and surpassed 100 RBIs for the fifth time. But while he stayed healthy all year, the Mets continued to be dogged by injuries, and they finished fourth in the NL East for the second year in a row. Though the young phenom has matured into a veteran, Wright is only now at the age where power hitters reach their prime, and the Mets will look to the Great Wright Hope to get the team back to its winning ways.

$ 24.95
GATE 43
SECTION FIELD
SEAT G8
SAZE354
3JUNE11

CAREER HIGHLIGHTS

- only Mets player ever to bat over .300 in five straight seasons (2005–09)
- won both the Silver Slugger and Gold Glove Awards in 2007 and 2008
- five-time NL All-Star (2006–10)

5 THIRD BASE

David WRIGHT

ryan ZIMMERMAN 11

WASHINGTON NATIONALS ◆ NL East

Ryan Zimmerman's path to the majors was amazingly smooth and swift. He was playing in his final year at the University of Virginia in 2005 when Washington selected him fourth overall in the draft. He immediately joined the Nationals' Class-A affiliate and needed all of four games to earn a promotion to Double-A, where he batted .373 with nine home runs in 63 matches.

Meanwhile, the Nationals were enjoying their inaugural year in Washington in 2005 after the franchise relocated from Montreal. They amazed everyone by hanging onto first place as late as July 24, and now they needed a third baseman down the stretch. In the offseason, the Nats had acquired Vinny Castilla, who was coming off a stellar campaign (35 home runs, 132 RBIs), but the veteran wasn't getting it done. So Zimmerman got the call, and in 20 games that September he batted .397 with 10 doubles. Not bad for a 20-year-old who had started the season in college and had never played a single game in Triple-A.

Nats manager Frank Robinson was even more impressed with Zimmerman's character. He was a coach's dream: hardworking, mature, confident without being cocky, and always eager to improve. The Nationals were so sure about their future star that they traded away Castilla and installed Zimmerman as their everyday third baseman in 2006.

Everyone expected Zimmerman to be solid defensively. Scouts described him as the next Scott Rolen and even

whispered the name of Brooks Robinson, who won 16 Gold Gloves with the Orioles in the 1960s and 1970s. Zimmerman could also hit for average, but no one was expecting him to be so deadly as a run producer. Usually slotted third or fifth in the lineup, he batted .323 with runners in scoring position, belted 20 home runs and amassed 110 RBIs. His 47 doubles were the second-highest ever by a freshman. Despite leading first-year players in almost all offensive categories, Zimmerman missed out on winning the NL Rookie of the Year, finishing four points behind Hanley Ramirez in one of the closest votes ever.

Several of Zimmerman's long balls that year came with a hefty dose of drama: his first career home run lit up Mets closer Billy Wagner and tied the game in the ninth. Then he beat the Yankees with a walk-off two-run shot on Father's Day, with his proud dad in attendance. He continued to pick his spots in 2007. His first two home runs of the season were both grand slams, one of them a game-winning blast in the bottom of the ninth. In all, he collected 18 game-winning RBIs in that campaign, one shy of the MLB lead.

In late May 2008, Zimmerman suffered the first significant injury of his career. While sliding into first

base, he tore the labrum in his left shoulder. He wound up on the sidelines for 48 games, but returned to bat .283 with 14 homers in the abbreviated campaign.

During the offseason, Zimmerman committed to a new regimen of healthy eating and reported to camp in 2009 in top shape and determined to have his best season to date. He came flying out of the blocks. In the third match, he began a 30-game hit streak that wasn't snapped until May 13. Then in July and August he strung together another 16-gamer. Playing his first full season at Nationals Park — and batting ahead of newly acquired slugger Adam Dunn — he swatted 33 homers and drove in 106 runs, picking up the Silver Slugger as the NL's best hitting third baseman. He also patrolled the hot corner with more confidence than ever. He led the majors in total chances and assists and earned his first Gold Glove, an award his fans felt was long overdue.

Zimmerman raised his average to a career-best .307 in 2010, and tallied 25 jacks and a .510 slugging percentage, good enough to win his second straight Silver Slugger. For a guy who was supposed to be a defensive specialist, Ryan Zimmerman has become a double threat and emerged as one of the finest two-way players in the game.

$ 24.95
GATE 25
SECTION CLUB
SEAT C24
J2MP222
18SEPT11

CAREER HIGHLIGHTS

- only the third NL player since 1954 to collect 100 RBIs in his rookie season (2006)
- two-time winner of the Silver Slugger award (2009–10)
- selected to NL All-Star Team in 2009

11 THIRD BASE

Ryan ZIMMERMAN

JASON KENDALL - Kansas City Royals

JOE MAUER - Minnesota Twins

BRIAN McCANN - Atlanta Braves

YADIER MOLINA - St. Louis Cardinals

KURT SUZUKI - Oakland Athletics

BACKSTOPS

jason KENDALL

18

If Jason Kendall's career had ended with the horrific injury he suffered on July 4, 1999, he would have been remembered only for his unrealized potential. Instead, the Iron Man of catchers is celebrated for more than a decade of accomplishments since that frightening afternoon at Three Rivers Stadium in Pittsburgh.

By his mid-20s, Kendall was arguably the best all-around catcher in the National League, and his hustle and spirit made him the heart of the Pittsburgh Pirates. He was an All-Star in his rookie season in 1996, and two years later he batted .327 with 36 doubles. Halfway through the 1999 campaign Kendall was hitting .332, with a .511 slugging percentage. When he wasn't preventing stolen bases — he'd gunned down 47 percent of potential thieves so far — he was stealing bases himself. Almost unheard of for a catcher, Kendall had already swiped 22 bags in half a season before that fateful game on Independence Day. Running hard after dropping down a bunt, Kendall stepped awkwardly on the edge of first base, dislocating and shattering his right angle. He stumbled to the ground and went into shock while teammates turned away from the sight of the bone jutting grotesquely through the skin.

Many who witnessed the injury thought Kendall might never play baseball again — or if he did, he'd never regain his speed. But the tough-as-nails catcher was back behind the plate on Opening Day 2000. Kendall was batting .321 on May 19 when the Pirates faced the Cardinals, and he smacked a two-run homer his first time up, then singled and doubled in his next two at-bats. He struck out in his next plate appearance, but got another opportunity in the eighth with two men on. Against the odds, he ripped a line drive into right center and legged out a triple, becoming the first Pirate to hit for the cycle at Three Rivers. Unafraid to test his rebuilt ankle, Kendall swiped another 22 bases that season, becoming the only catcher in history to steal 20 or more in three seasons.

CAREER HIGHLIGHTS

- one of only five catchers in MLB history to play in 2,000 games

- since 1900, leads all MLB catchers with 189 career stolen bases

- one of only four active players with more bases on balls than strikeouts over a career of at least 10 seasons (721 walks, 686 strikeouts)

18   CATCHER

Jason KENDALL

Kendall had one of his best offensive years in 2003, when he batted .325 with a career-high 191 hits, including a 23-game hitting streak. He followed that up with a .319 campaign with the Pirates in 2004 before being traded to the Oakland A's. The Athletics were attracted to patient contact hitters like Kendall, who could not only hit for average, but regularly walked more times than he struck out. (He also holds the painful distinction of leading all active players with 254 hit-by-pitches.) Kendall was often the A's leadoff batter and started more than 140 games behind the plate during each of his first two years in Oakland, and by the end of 2006, he still owned a .300 career batting average over 11 seasons.

After a decade in which he never saw the postseason, Kendall suddenly found himself playing October baseball three years in a row with three different teams. The first time was with the Athletics, who returned to the playoffs in 2006 and swept the Twins in the ALDS. Kendall batted .294 in the Championship Series that year, but the Tigers won it in four games. The following season, the A's sent Kendall to the Chicago Cubs, who won the NL Central, but Kendall watched his club lose

three straight in the Division Series. A free agent that offseason, he signed with the Milwaukee Brewers and again helped his club win the NL Central. But not only did the Brewers lose the NLDS in four games, Kendall struggled mightily at the plate, managing two singles in 14 trips.

Kendall's bat is not nearly the danger it was in his prime, but his durability remains. He caught a career-high 1,328 innings for the Brewers in 2008 and led the National League by throwing out 43 percent of attempted base stealers. He caught another 1,160 innings in 2009, and in a game against the Cardinals on May 19, he smacked a single in the fourth inning for his 2,000th career hit.

Before the 2010 season, Kendall returned to the American League when he inked a two-year deal with the Kansas City Royals. The oldest player on the club, he was leading the league with 118 games caught on August 30, and had even stolen 12 bases, his highest total since 2002. But that's when the Royals announced that Kendall had a badly damaged rotator cuff. It turned out he had suffered the injury back on July 17 and played through the pain — incredibly, the very next day he had gunned down three runners trying to steal. Now doctors decided he would need surgery, and they said the recovery would take eight to ten months. Of course, Jason Kendall has heard that before.

joe MAUER

MINNESOTA TWINS ◆ AL Central

The Minnesota Twins' catcher is no ordinary Joe. Indeed, there simply has never been another major-league backstop like Joseph Patrick Mauer. To begin with, his body appears all wrong for the position: rather than having the short, stocky build of most catchers, Mauer is a towering six-foot-five. And while managers are usually happy if their catcher can hit .260, Joe Mauer is a three-time batting champion.

Mauer is a hometown hero in Minneapolis–St. Paul. He grew up a few miles from the Metrodome and his accomplishments in high school are legendary. He was twice named to the All-State basketball team, and in 2001 he was the first player ever to be named by *USA Today* as the country's best high school player in both baseball and football. When Minnesota had the first overall draft pick that year, they pounced on Mauer and signed him immediately.

In 2003, Mauer batted .338 in the minors and the Twins decided that he was ready to be their starting catcher the following year, even though he would still be a week shy of his 21st birthday on Opening Day. The club's confidence in Mauer was so great that they traded away A.J. Pierzynski — a .300 hitter in the two previous seasons — to make room for him. His much ballyhooed debut in 2004 featured a terrifying moment. In his third big-league game, he was chasing a foul popup when he suffered a torn meniscus in his left knee. All of a sudden, Mauer's catching career looked like it might be threatened before it had begun. He returned in June and played another six weeks, but when the injury did not heal properly, the Twins pulled the plug on his season. Mauer was too young and too valuable to take chances with.

The knee appeared to be fine in 2005. Mauer caught 116 games and led the Twins' starting nine with a .294 average and was outstanding defensively, using his athleticism to pounce on bunts and his rocket arm to gun down 43 percent of would-be thieves. A

humble and low-key young man, it took him some time to be assertive with pitchers, especially superstars like Johan Santana. But eventually, as his confidence grew, he proved adept at calling for the right pitches in every situation.

With hopes raised for 2006, Mauer hit .319 in the first month, upped that to .386 in May and then attacked the ball at a 42-for-93 clip in June to push his average to .378 by the All-Star break. Derek Jeter overtook in mid-September, but Mauer surged ahead in the final weeks to capture the batting title with a .347 mark. His 79 walks gave him an OBP of .429, and he struck out a mere 54 times. It was one of the best offensive seasons ever by a young catcher.

Mauer's 2007 campaign was disappointing on a number of levels. The Twins never took a serious run at the division title, and as the defending batting champ battled a pair of leg injuries, some of his teammates whispered to the press that he seemed unwilling to play through pain. Limited to 109 games, Mauer still managed to hit .293.

The whispers stopped in 2008 when Mauer won his second batting title with a .328 average and collected 85 RBIs, his highest total to date. He also threw out 36 percent of potential base stealers and committed just three errors and four passed balls in more than 1,200 innings behind the plate, good enough to be awarded his first Gold Glove to go along with his second Silver Slugger.

Another injury forced Mauer to miss all of April in 2009, but he returned to have a record-setting month. He homered in his first at bat, and then hit 10 more long balls and drove in 32 runs in May alone, after hitting no more than 13 homers in any previous season. When he started for the American League in the All-Star Game, he was batting .373 with 15 homers and 49 RBIs in only 64 games. With another power surge in August, Mauer finished the year atop the league in batting average (.365), on-base percentage (.444) and slugging (.587), the first player to accomplish that trifecta in 29 years. The Twins nailed down the AL Central in a one-game playoff against the Tigers, but they continued their pattern of early exits in the postseason. Mauer's .417 average couldn't prevent a three-game sweep by the Yankees in the ALDS. The catcher consoled himself in the offseason with his first American League MVP Award.

While his power numbers returned to normal levels (nine home runs), Mauer continued to swing a hot stick in 2010, placing third in the batting race with a .327 average. He also seemed to like the dimensions of Minnesota's new Target Field, as he lashed a career-best 43 doubles, 13 more than in his MVP season. He started 107 games at catcher and secured his third straight Gold Glove.

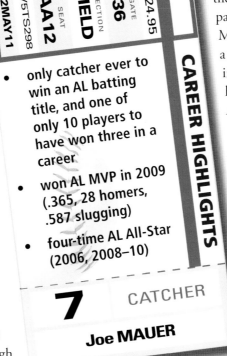

$ 24.95
GATE 36
SECTION FIELD
SEAT AA12
V5TS298
2MAY11

CAREER HIGHLIGHTS

- only catcher ever to win an AL batting title, and one of only 10 players to have won three in a career
- won AL MVP in 2009 (.365, 28 homers, .587 slugging)
- four-time AL All-Star (2006, 2008–10)

7 CATCHER

Joe MAUER

brian McCANN

ATLANTA BRAVES ◆ NL East

When Brian McCann began his journey through the Atlanta Braves' farm system, he had the advantage of being a hometown favorite. The six-foot-three catcher grew up in the Atlanta area. As a kid, he'd watched Bobby Cox lead the club to a streak of 14 consecutive postseason appearances that was still alive when McCann joined the club.

The 21-year-old McCann made his big-league debut on June 10, 2005, singled in his first at-bat, and then knocked his first home run the next day. He batted .278 in that abbreviated season — including a .347 clip with runners on base — and did an outstanding job of handling the Braves' pitching staff. John Smoltz was so impressed that he asked to have McCann as his battery mate every time he went to the mound. The honeymoon continued into the postseason, as McCann caught Smoltz's Game 2 start against the Astros in the NLDS. In the second inning of that match, he ripped a 2–0 pitch from Roger Clemens over the center field wall for a three-run homer to lead his club to a 7–1 romp. Unfortunately for McCann, that would be the only game Atlanta won in the 2005 playoffs.

The Braves handed McCann the full-time catcher's job in 2006. He responded with a torrid couple of months, and on May 20 he was leading the National League with a .350 average. He missed two weeks with an ankle sprain after a collision at home plate, but he continued pounding the ball after his return, and during one stretch in July he stroked home runs in five consecutive games. On the season, McCann posted a .333 average with 24 home runs, 93 RBIs and a .961 OPS, a remarkable achievement for a 22-year-old catcher, and enough to earn him the Silver Slugger. The taint on McCann's breakout season, however, was that the Braves' run of consecutive division titles came to an end.

After batting .345 in the first three weeks of the 2007 season, McCann was struck on the ring finger of his left hand while attempting to lay down a sacrifice bunt. A couple of weeks later he aggravated the injury when an opponent's swing hit him in the glove. By May 19, his average had dropped almost 70 points and it hovered around .270 the rest of the way, though he still finished with 38 doubles, 18 home runs and 92 RBIs in 132 games.

In the offseason, McCann had Lasik surgery to correct the vision in his left eye, and everything started well in the 2008 campaign. He batted .301 with 23 home runs, a career-high 42 doubles, and 87 RBIs, picking up his second Silver Slugger Award. But McCann complained of continued eye problems early in 2009 and was hitting a paltry .195 at the end of April. He spent time on the DL and returned in May wearing glasses, which were awkward under his catcher's mask, but did improve his performance with the bat. Though McCann's average fell to .281 on the year, he still knocked in a personal-best 94 RBIs, leading all other Braves players by a wide margin.

McCann had laser surgery again before the 2010 campaign in an effort to correct the eye problems for good. He didn't see the ball well at all during the first six weeks of the season, but then he batted .316 over July and August and matched his previous year's 21 home runs. His mid-season hot streak continued in the All-Star Game. With the American League leading 1–0 in the seventh and looking to win its 14th consecutive Midsummer Classic, McCann came to the dish with the bases loaded to face White Sox reliever Matt Thornton. The catcher scorched a line drive into the right field corner that cleared the bases and gave the National League a 3–1 victory and won McCann the All-Star MVP Award.

The Braves won 91 games in 2010 and finished second in the NL East, securing the wild card on the last day of the season. Atlanta hoped for a little postseason magic in Bobby Cox's final fling, and McCann did his part by batting .429 in the NLDS against the San Francisco Giants. His sixth-inning home run off Madison Bumgarner in Game 4 broke a 1–1 tie and gave the Braves hopes of staying alive, but the Giants responded with a pair in the seventh and clinched the series that night.

The Braves are now entering a new era in Atlanta under manager Fredi Gonzalez. With his vision problems behind him, McCann has his sights set on a new dynasty.

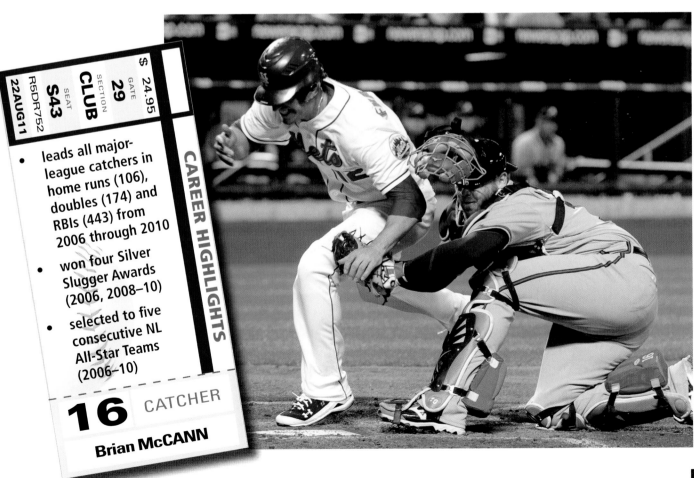

$ 24.95
GATE 29
SECTION CLUB
SEAT S43
R5DR752
22AUG11

CAREER HIGHLIGHTS

- leads all major-league catchers in home runs (106), doubles (174) and RBIs (443) from 2006 through 2010

- won four Silver Slugger Awards (2006, 2008–10)

- selected to five consecutive NL All-Star Teams (2006–10)

16 CATCHER

Brian McCANN

yadier MOLINA

Casual baseball fans don't always appreciate the subtle skills of a great defensive catcher — deterring base stealers, pitch selection and location, working with a pitching staff — but insiders know these are essential ingredients of a winning team. And no man in the mask is better at these areas of the game than Yadier Molina.

Yadier Molina was born in Bayamon, Puerto Rico, in 1982. His brothers Bengie and Jose (eight and seven years older, respectively) had already debuted as big-league catchers when the 18-year-old Yadier signed with the St. Louis Cardinals. While the youngest Molina was playing Class-A ball in 2002, Bengie and Jose were sharing the catching duties with the Anaheim Angels, who won the World Series that year. While baseball has seen other trios of talented brothers — notably the DiMaggios and the Alous — no family had ever produced three catchers, let alone three siblings with World Series rings. Yadier hoped he would change that some day.

When Molina joined the Cardinals in 2004, he was the backup for Mike Matheny, one of the best defensive catchers of his generation. The 21-year-old apprentice played in 39 games and quickly staked a claim behind the plate, gunning down 8 of 16 attempted base stealers and, in one August game, making two gutsy putouts at home, including a thunderous collision with the Pirates' Ty Wigginton. Molina's message was clear: if you want to score, you need to get through me first.

Matheny left for the Giants in 2005, and Molina inherited the full-time receiver's job. That season he threw out 17 of 31 attempted base stealers to lead the majors — the small number of attempts suggests most would-be thieves didn't even bother testing his arm. Molina missed a month with a fractured wrist, but he returned to help the Cardinals nail down the division title, and caught all nine of the Redbirds' postseason games. He chipped in with a .286 playoff average

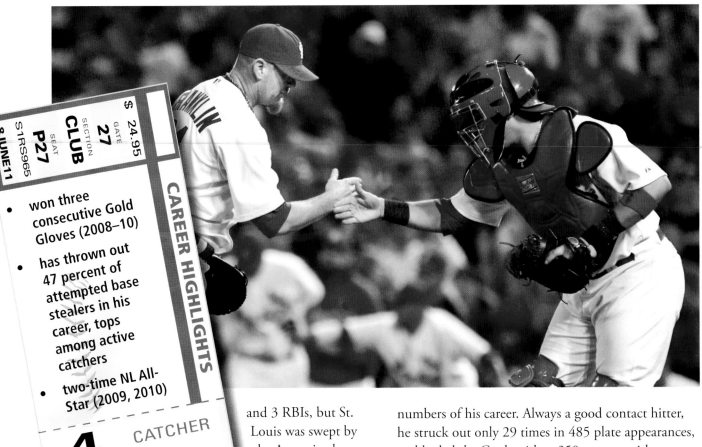

CAREER HIGHLIGHTS

- won three consecutive Gold Gloves (2008–10)
- has thrown out 47 percent of attempted base stealers in his career, tops among active catchers
- two-time NL All-Star (2009, 2010)

CATCHER

4 Yadier MOLINA

and 3 RBIs, but St. Louis was swept by the Astros in the NLCS.

The Cardinals snuck into the 2006 postseason with a mediocre 83–78 record, and Molina's .216 average was 40 points lower than any other regular on the team. That's what made his playoff performance so magically unexpected: he led all Cardinals batters with a .358 average, 19 hits and 29 total bases, and was second with 8 RBIs. When the Cardinals squared off against the Mets in the Championship Series, it came down to the ninth inning in Game 7. The teams were deadlocked 1–1 when Scott Rolen singled with one out off Aaron Heilman. Molina had six home runs all season and was hardly a power threat, but Heilman left his first pitch up in the strike zone and the light-hitting catcher ripped it over the wall for a two-run homer that sent the Cards to the Fall Classic for the second year in a row. Molina batted .412 in the series, as St. Louis defeated Detroit in five games. Four years after Bengie and Jose had won it all with the Angels, Yadier, too, had a World Series ring on his finger.

The Gold Glove selections aren't supposed to be influenced by offense, but it's certainly easier to get noticed if you can hit. In 2008, Molina batted .304 with a .392 slugging percentage and 56 RBIs, the best

numbers of his career. Always a good contact hitter, he struck out only 29 times in 485 plate appearances, and he led the Cards with a .350 average with runners in scoring position. He continued to be an impassable barrier at home. In the ninth inning of a tie game with the Phillies in June, Molina tagged out Eric Bruntlett, who was charging in from third, despite being knocked senseless in the collision. The catcher had to be driven from the field on a stretcher and missed three games with a concussion. Then in September he stood up to the Cubs' Ted Lilly in another home-plate tackle, suffering a quadriceps injury that effectively ended his season. For those heroics and his daily masterwork behind the dish, Molina finally won his first Gold Glove Award.

Molina was the starting receiver for the NL All-Star Game in both 2009 and 2010 as he cemented his reputation as the best catcher in the game. In the first of those years, he also became the first Cardinals catcher in history to appear in four postseasons — he batted .308 against the Dodgers in a losing cause in the NLDS. In 2010, he upped his career high in RBIs to 62 by making the most of his big swings: although he hit just six home runs, two were grand slams. Not only did he receive his third Gold Glove that year, but the analysts at the Fielding Bible Awards made him the first unanimous choice as the best defensive player at any position. To the seamheads who understand the subtleties of baseball, Yadier Molina is a perfect 10.

kurt SUZUKI

OAKLAND ATHLETICS ◆ AL West

When Kurt Suzuki goes into his home-run trot, fans will notice a puka shell necklace bouncing around on his neck. The young catcher started wearing the necklace to remind him of home when he left Wailuku, Hawaii, to attend college at California State University, Fullerton. The school didn't offer him a scholarship, but he made the team as a walk-on and eventually blossomed into one of the finest collegiate catchers in the country.

In June of his senior year, the Oakland A's drafted Suzuki in the second round. A couple of weeks later, he found himself in the finals of the 2004 College World Series against the University of Texas. Fullerton won the first game of the best-of-three, but trailed 2–0 in the seventh inning of Game 2. They had just rallied to tie the score when Suzuki came to the plate with runners at first and second and two out. He lashed a line drive into left field to bring home the run that would give Fullerton the college championship. That huge hit

helped establish Suzuki's reputation for driving in big runs. He reaffirmed it in 2006 while playing for USA Baseball's Olympic qualifying team, when he slugged a walk-off home run to beat Brazil.

The A's don't usually let talented young players languish in the minor leagues, and Suzuki was no exception. He played the 2006 season in the Double-A Texas League, where he cut down over 47 percent of attempted base stealers, and started the following campaign in Triple-A. But by June 2007, the A's were ready for a look at their 23-year-old prospect, who was slated to replace veteran catcher Jason Kendall. The organization must have been impressed, because a month later they traded Kendall and made the rookie their everyday backstop.

In 2008, Suzuki's first full season, he led the league in games caught (141) and batted a team-best .279. He also continued to display an ability to hit in the clutch. In one June game against the Marlins, he opened the scoring with a two-run homer, regained the lead with a two-run double after the Marlins went up 5–4, and then won it in the 11th with a walk-off double. A couple of weeks later, he came off the bench with two outs in the ninth and hit a game-tying home run against the Mariners. And in August, he belted a pinch-hit game-winning homer against the White Sox, then beat the Twins later in the month with another walk-off pinch hit.

Somewhat surprisingly, Suzuki has emerged as the top offensive threat in an admittedly weak Athletics lineup. In 2009, he collected 37 doubles, an Oakland record for catchers, and led the team with 88 RBIs, the first time since 1944 that a receiver had paced the A's in that category. His average dropped to .242 in 2010, but he again led the team with 71 runs driven in.

Although he's a .264 lifetime hitter, Suzuki makes the most of his at-bats. Over his career, his average is almost 40 points higher with runners in scoring position than with the bases empty, and he's hit .417 with a man on third and less than two out — one of those stats that managers love. He's an outstanding contact hitter who strikes out only once in every 11 at-bats. If there's one hole in his game, it's his recent reluctance to take walks. The A's organization has long stressed the importance of working the count, and in the minors Suzuki was as good as anyone at drawing bases on balls. In 2009 and 2010, however, his OBP was well below the league average.

As effective as Suzuki has been with the bat, his real value is his defense. In 2010, *Baseball America* named him the second-best defensive catcher in the American League, behind only Joe Mauer. He's extraordinarily good at calling games for Oakland's young guns, including Trevor Cahill, Gio Gonzalez, Dallas Braden and Brett Anderson. Athletics pitchers had a 3.27 ERA with him catching in 2010, the lowest in the American League.

So far, Suzuki's tenure in the big leagues has coincided with his team's decline. After a string of five trips to the postseason in seven years, the A's haven't finished above .500 since 2006. But Oakland looks like a team on the rise, thanks to outstanding talent on the mound and a gifted catcher who hasn't yet reached his prime.

$ 24.95
GATE 36
SECTION FIELD
SEAT J67
B6DT384
4OCT11

CAREER HIGHLIGHTS

- led the AL in games caught in 2008 and 2009
- only A's catcher to lead his team in RBIs twice (2009 and 2010)
- has collected eight walk-off hits since 2008, tops in the AL

8   CATCHER

Kurt SUZUKI

ADAM DUNN - Chicago White Sox

VLADIMIR GUERRERO - Baltimore Orioles

VICTOR MARTINEZ - Detroit Tigers

DAVID ORTIZ - Boston Red Sox

JIM THOME - Minnesota Twins

BATMEN

adam
DUNN

32

CHICAGO WHITE SOX ◆ AL Central

No one will ever accuse Adam Dunn of being an all-around player. He's a career .250 hitter who has had three seasons with at least 190 strikeouts. He hasn't stolen a base since August 2008. He led National League left fielders in errors four times. But there is one thing Dunn can do with the best players in the game, and that is pound the daylights out of a baseball. Since 2004, he has never hit fewer than 38 home runs in any season.

Growing up in Houston, Dunn seemed destined for a career on the gridiron. He was a star quarterback in high school, and baseball was something of an afterthought. When he became eligible for the MLB draft, teams were afraid to waste a pick on him, figuring he wouldn't sign. But the Cincinnati Reds eventually took him 50th overall in the 1998 entry draft and worked out an arrangement that allowed him to play football at the University of Texas. Eventually Dunn realized his future was on the diamond, and he set about punishing minor-league pitchers.

Cincinnati wasn't planning to rush Dunn's development, but in 2001 he hit 20 home runs in 50 games in Triple-A. The Reds, meanwhile, were hobbled by injuries, so in July they decided to plug a hole with the 21-year-old outfielder.

$ 24.95
GATE 21
SECTION UPPER
SEAT A14
G2BV/256
7MAY11

CAREER HIGHLIGHTS

- eighth player in MLB history to record five straight seasons with 40 home runs (2004–2008)
- seven seasons with a slugging percentage of at least .500
- third among all active hitters with one home run every 14.05 at-bats

32 DESIGNATED HITTER

Adam DUNN

In his first 66 games in the bigs, Dunn belted 19 home runs and slugged .578. That was all the Reds needed to see: he easily made the team the following spring and became an everyday player in 2002, patrolling the outfield and playing first base.

By 2004, Dunn had earned a reputation as one of the most feared power hitters in the game. During one game that year, he blasted a pitch right out of Cincinnati's Great American Ball Park. According to ESPN's Jayson Stark, the ball travelled some 535 feet on the fly, then rolled another 200 feet to the Ohio River, "which meant it was hit in Ohio and came to rest in Kentucky." The only number more remarkable than his 46 home runs that year was his 195 strikeouts — a new major league record.

Dunn posted solidly consistent numbers from 2005 through 2008: he hit exactly 40 home runs and drove in about 100 runs in each season. In August 2008, Dunn was shipped to Arizona, where the Diamondbacks were holding down first place in the NL West. After years with the underperforming Reds, Dunn looked forward to getting his first opportunity to play in the postseason. But a prolonged skid in September allowed the Dodgers to overtake the Diamondbacks, and when the season was over, Dunn became a free agent and signed with the Washington Nationals.

Dunn split his time between left field and first base in 2009 before making the reluctant move to full-time infielder in 2010. At the plate he continued his remarkably consistent slugging, posting two almost identical seasons with the Nationals: 38 home runs in both 2009 and 2010, with 105 and 103 RBIs, respectively. A free agent again following the 2010 campaign, Dunn inked a four-year deal with the Chicago White Sox. He'll likely be even more successful in the American League, where he'll make an ideal designated hitter.

Dunn has his critics, to be sure. One telling statistic is that over his career he has put the ball in play in only about half of his plate appearances; the rest of the time he walks, strikes out or hits a home run. But a close look at his performance turns up some interesting facts. He is unusually good against southpaws (rare for a left-handed batter), and is often among the league leaders in pitches per plate appearance, a trait that can wear down opposing hurlers. He's also been extremely durable. Since injuring his thumb in 2003, he's been in the lineup just about every day for seven long seasons.

Most surprising is his ability to get on base despite his low batting average and extremely high strikeout rate. Dunn has drawn over 100 walks in seven of his 10 seasons: his 128 bases on balls in 2002 were the most ever by a player under 23 years old, and he led the league with 122 in 2008. That willingness to take a walk has allowed him to compile a career on-base percentage of .381 — higher than Ichiro Suzuki's. Who would you rather have at the plate with the bases loaded?

vladimir GUERRERO 27

BALTIMORE ORIOLES ◆ AL East

During his five years in right field with the Montreal Expos, Vladimir Guerrero thrived in obscurity. From 1998 through 2002, Guerrero averaged .325 with 39 home runs and 117 RBIs, yet he went mostly unnoticed. In 2000, he had a phenomenal campaign, with a .345 average, 44 homers, 123 RBIs and a slugging percentage of .664, yet he finished sixth in the MVP voting. Guerrero's profile only changed after he signed with the Angels prior to the 2004 season. Although his numbers were merely average for him (.337, 39 homers, 126 RBIs), he won MVP honors that year, and finally got recognized as one of the greatest all-around hitters of his generation.

Guerrero, born in the Dominican Republic in 1976, became a star with the Expos at age 23, when he batted .324 with 38 homers in his first full season. When he surpassed .300 with at least 30 homers and 100 RBIs in the next two campaigns as well, he became just the fourth player in MLB history to do so three times before age 25 — the others are Hall of Famers Ted Williams, Jimmie Foxx and Joe DiMaggio. (Albert Pujols would later join the group.) Guerrero reached those milestones five more times by 2006.

Vlad is not your stereotypical slugger. He doesn't whiff very often, and in several seasons he has collected more walks than strikeouts. Yet he's anything but disciplined: he'll flail at anything from his shoe tops to his eyes — and he'll hit it hard. More than once he's tallied base hits on pitches that bounced in front of the plate, and he's hit home runs off pitches an inch from the dirt, or at his shoulders.

Guerrero finally got a chance to play on a contender when he signed as a free agent with Anaheim. The Angels trailed Oakland in the AL West by three games in the final week of 2004, but rallied to win the division, thanks in part to Guerrero's 15-for-28 (.536) clip with six home runs and 11 RBIs. The Red Sox swept the Angels in the ALDS that year, and Guerrero

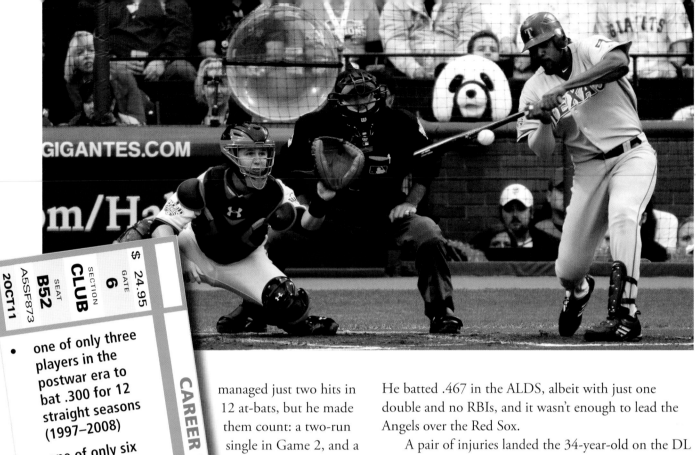

CAREER HIGHLIGHTS

- one of only three players in the postwar era to bat .300 for 12 straight seasons (1997–2008)

- one of only six players in history with 400 home runs and a career batting average of .320

- selected to nine All-Star Teams between 1999 and 2010

27 DESIGNATED HITTER

Vladimir GUERRERO

managed just two hits in 12 at-bats, but he made them count: a two-run single in Game 2, and a game-tying grand slam in the final match.

With his big bat and his bigger smile, Guerrero won over Angels fans during the next two seasons. He hit .317 with 32 home runs and 108 RBIs in 2005, and .329 with 33 homers and 116 RBIs in 2006. Ironically, Guerrero's lowest power numbers came in 2007, the year he won the Home Run Derby at the All-Star Game. Although he pounded 17 balls into the stands during the derby on July 9, he went homerless from June 24 until August 2, the longest drought of his career, and finished the year with 27. (He still batted his usual .325 and drove in 125 runs.) Vlad performed poorly in the 2007 postseason, when he managed two singles in 10 at-bats as the Angels were again swept by the Red Sox.

Guerrero collected his 2,000th career hit early in 2008, and joined Lou Gehrig as the only players to hit at least .300 with 25 home runs in 11 straight seasons. He finally snapped his postseason slump in 2008, too.

He batted .467 in the ALDS, albeit with just one double and no RBIs, and it wasn't enough to lead the Angels over the Red Sox.

A pair of injuries landed the 34-year-old on the DL twice in 2009, and he was unable to maintain his streak of 25-homer seasons. His average also slipped under .300 for the first time in his career. But Guerrero had his best postseason to date. In Game 3 of the ALDS against the arch-rival Red Sox, he won the deciding Game 3 when he lined a two-run single off Jonathan Papelbon with two outs in the ninth. He was even better in the ALCS — he batted .370 with a home run and five RBIs against the Yankees — but the Angels dropped the series in six games.

When Guerrero's five-year deal with the Angels expired after the 2009 season, the slugger inked a deal with the Texas Rangers, adding another bat to an already impressive lineup. He stayed healthy, played in 152 games and put up classic Vlad numbers: .300 average, 29 homers and 115 RBIs. After a two-year hiatus, he once again earned an All-Star selection (his ninth), and picked up his first Silver Slugger at the DH position (his eighth overall).

Back in the playoffs for the sixth time in seven years, Guerrero smacked a two-run double in the deciding Game 6 of the ALCS and helped send the Rangers to their first World Series. But when he was forced to patrol right field in Game 1 of the Fall Classic, he made two costly errors. Manager Ron Washington left him out of the lineup in Game 2. When the series returned to Arlington, Guerrero went 0-for-10 in the final three games.

victor
MARTINEZ

41

During 2010, Victor Martinez spent most of his playing time with the Boston Red Sox, behind the plate, but when the Detroit Tigers signed him before the 2011 season, they announced that he would primarily be their designated hitter. It wasn't the first time a team had asked Martinez to change positions. In the 2009 campaign, which he split between the Red Sox and the Cleveland Indians, he shuffled between catcher and first base. In fact, when the Indians signed him out of Venezuela back in 1996, the 18-year-old fancied himself a shortstop. In every case, the reason for the positional shifts was the same: find a way to get this guy's bat in the lineup every day.

Martinez earned the catcher's job in Cleveland in 2004 and promptly stamped his name on it. The switch hitter batted .283 and led all major-league catchers with 23 home runs and 108 RBIs, tying Ivan Rodriguez for the Silver Slugger Award in his first full season. He earned a reputation as a patient contact hitter — he drew 60 walks and fanned only 69 times — and as a reliable batter in the clutch. Martinez hit .319 with men on base (his lifetime average in that situation is .312), and his coaches and teammates also praised his work ethic and his leadership qualities around the clubhouse.

On the strength of a stellar second half (his .380 average after the break was tops in the majors), Martinez batted .305 in 2005 and paced the Indians as they took a serious charge at the White Sox for the AL Central crown, though the Tribe was unable to catch the eventual World Series champs. He upped his average to a career-best .316 in 2006 and drove in 93 runs. Usually a slow starter, he bucked the trend by hitting .395 that April, reaching base safely in every game during the month.

When the Indians won the division title in 2007, it was Martinez who keyed the offense. Batting cleanup behind Travis Hafner, the catcher led his team in almost every category: average (.301), home runs (25), RBIs (114), slugging (.505) and OPS (.879). He also threw out 30 percent of runners who tried to steal against him, double his rate of 2006. Martinez continued his hot hitting in his first postseason, posting a .318 average, knocking a home run in each series and driving in seven runs in 11 games, before Cleveland was eliminated by the Red Sox in the ALCS.

The 2008 campaign was a virtual write-off for Martinez. He batted .350 in April, but by mid-May he was feeling a shooting pain in his right elbow. He tried to play through the discomfort, but by mid-June he was unable to swing a bat. Martinez had arthroscopic surgery to repair the elbow and didn't return until late August.

The Indians began using Martinez at first base and catcher more or less equally in 2009, and he regained his form at the plate. He was selected to his third All-Star team, and by the end of July he was batting a solid .284 with 15 home runs. Just before the trade deadline, the Tribe swung a deal that sent Martinez to Boston in return for three pitchers. Like the Indians, the Red Sox also used their new acquisition at both first base and behind the plate, and he swung a red-hot bat down the stretch. Martinez batted .336 and drove in 41 runs in 56 games, helping the Sox capture the AL wild card. He was the starting catcher for all three ALDS

games against the Angels, but he managed just two hits in 11 at-bats, as the Red Sox were swept in three straight.

With Jason Varitek either injured or struggling with the bat for much of 2010, Martinez once again found himself as an everyday catcher. He, too, spent time on the DL, missing almost all of July after being hit with two foul tips in the same game and suffering a fracture in his left thumb. Despite the injury, in 127 games he batted over .300 for the fifth time in his career, and pounded another 20 homers, tied for first among backstops. He was particularly lethal from the right side of the plate, leading the majors with a .400 average and a .742 slugging percentage against left-handed pitching.

Martinez became a free agent after the 2010 season and agreed to a four-year deal with the Tigers. With young Alex Avila looking like the team's catcher of the future and Miguel Cabrera holding down the job at first, Martinez may see little time in the field, but he's sure to add some pop to the batting order.

$ 24.95
GATE 15
SECTION FIELD
SEAT J22
S3SD469
29JUNE11

CAREER HIGHLIGHTS

- owns a .300 career batting average in over 1,000 games
- has five seasons with 20+ homers and three with over 100 RBIs
- four-time AL All-Star (2004, 2007, 2009, 2010)

41 DESIGNATED HITTER

Victor MARTINEZ

david ORTIZ

David Ortiz's emergence as one of the most deadly hitters in the American League was entirely unexpected. Drafted by the Seattle Mariners in 1992, he was dealt to the Minnesota Twins four years later as an afterthought in a deal to acquire journeyman Dave Hollins. He played 86 games with the Twins in 1998, but the team demoted him to Triple-A the following year. For the next three unremarkable seasons, Ortiz played sporadically, and the Twins saw no place for him in their future. In December 2002, they tried to trade him, and when no one showed interest, they simply released him.

The Red Sox decided to take a chance on the 27-year-old who had a history of injuries, no speed, a below-average glove, and whose most productive season was 20 homers and 75 RBIs. By the middle of May 2003, the cast-off was batting .205 with a single home run and he was asking to be traded. But the Bosox didn't oblige him. Instead, they dumped the troublesome Shea Hillenbrand and made room for Ortiz in the everyday lineup. He embraced his new role as full-time DH, and from July onward he slugged 28 home runs, helping Boston turn things around and win the wild card race. Over the next seven seasons, Big Papi would become one of the most beloved figures in Red Sox Nation.

Hitting third in front of Manny Ramirez in 2004, Ortiz was part of a devastating one-two punch. He led the AL with 91 extra-base hits, including 41 homers, and drove in 139 runs. Once again securing the wild card spot, the Red Sox faced the Anaheim Angels in the ALDS. They won the first two games and completed the sweep when Ortiz homered in the 10th inning to end Game 3.

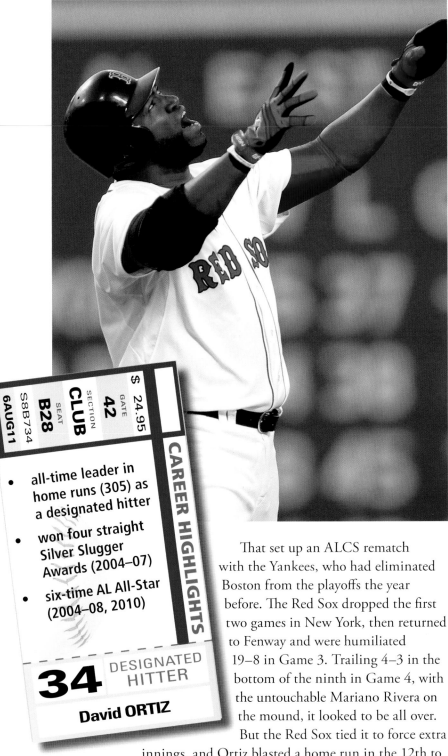

Cardinals, claiming their first World Series championship in 86 years.

Amazingly, Ortiz actually improved his numbers in 2005, upping his home run total to 47 and collecting a league-leading 148 RBIs. He followed that up with an AL-best 54 homers in 2006, setting a Red Sox record and a new mark for designated hitters. He added to his reputation as a peerless clutch hitter with five walk-off hits, including three game-ending homers.

Ortiz was bothered by a sore knee in 2007, but still managed to bat .332 with 52 doubles (both career highs) and slug 35 home runs. He was red-hot when it mattered: he compiled a 1.341 OPS in September, as the Red Sox locked up first place in the AL East. Big Papi didn't have any of his signature walk-off moments in the postseason, but he batted .370 with six doubles, three homers, 10 RBIs and an OBP of .525 as Boston won its second World Series in four years.

Since 2008, Ortiz has battled nagging injuries that have reduced his playing time and his effectiveness. He missed over 50 games in 2008 and batted .264 with just 23 home runs, and his average fell to .238 in 2009. He also seems to have lost some of his postseason mojo. In the 2008 and 2009 playoffs, he was a combined 9-for-55 (.166) with one home run, although that one long ball was a three-run blast that helped the Red Sox come back from a 7–0 deficit in Game 5 of the ALCS against Tampa Bay.

Big Papi rebounded in 2010, overcoming a slow start to bat .270 with 32 homers and 102 RBIs, matching the record for most 100-RBI seasons by a DH (five). He also extended another of his all-time marks on July 31, when he came to bat in the bottom of the ninth with the Red Sox trailing the Tigers 4–2. Ortiz lined a bases-clearing double into left-center for the 18th walk-off hit of his career, cementing his reputation as one of the greatest clutch hitters in Red Sox history.

That set up an ALCS rematch with the Yankees, who had eliminated Boston from the playoffs the year before. The Red Sox dropped the first two games in New York, then returned to Fenway and were humiliated 19–8 in Game 3. Trailing 4–3 in the bottom of the ninth in Game 4, with the untouchable Mariano Rivera on the mound, it looked to be all over. But the Red Sox tied it to force extra innings, and Ortiz blasted a home run in the 12th to stave off elimination. In the next match, Ortiz homered in the eighth to help the Sox erase a 4–2 Yankees lead and force extra innings again. In the bottom of the 14th, with two outs and two men on, Ortiz lined a single to center field for his second straight walk-off hit and his third of the playoffs. (No one else has recorded three walk-off hits in a postseason career, let alone in one year.) Boston completed the most improbable comeback in baseball history by winning the next two games to oust the Yankees, and Ortiz was an easy choice for series MVP. The Red Sox then went on to sweep the St. Louis

jim THOME

MINNESOTA TWINS ◆ AL Central

With 499 home runs already under his belt, Jim Thome decided that the next one should be special. It was 2007, Thome's second season with the Chicago White Sox, and he had already belted 27 long balls by September 16, when the Angels were visiting U.S. Cellular Field. With the score tied 7–7 in the bottom of the ninth, Thome turned on a full-count fastball and hit a bomb over the center field wall to win the game with the 500th home run of his Hall of Fame career.

Jim Thome was born in Peoria, Illinois, into a blue-collar baseball family that taught him the value of hard work. He was drafted as a corner infielder by the Cleveland Indians way back in 1989 and bounced between the big leagues and the minors until the Tribe made him their everyday third baseman in 1994. The following season, Thome hit .314 with 25 home runs as the Indians won 100 games and their first American League pennant since 1954.

As a third baseman, Thome won his first Silver Slugger in 1996, when he belted 38 home runs and had an OBP of .450 — thanks to a .311 batting average coupled with 123 bases on balls. Just 25 years old, Thome was already showing the selective eye that would eventually make him tops among all active players in walks.

Between 1999 and 2001, Thome established himself as one of the greatest power hitters in franchise history, with home run totals of 33, 37 and 49 during those years. His most fearsome performance came in 2002, when he batted .304, launched a franchise-record 52 homers and led the league with a .677 slugging percentage and an OPS of 1.122. The slugger was a big part of the Indians' resurgence, as the team reached the postseason six times from 1995 to 2001 after decades of futility, and he also earned a reputation for October heroics. Thome blasted 17 postseason home runs with

CAREER HIGHLIGHTS

- ranks eighth all-time with 589 career home runs

- has a career OBP of .404 and ranks ninth all-time with 1,679 bases on balls

- owns 17 postseason home runs, one shy of the all-time record

25 DESIGNATED HITTER

Jim THOME

the Indians, and he's the only player to have socked two playoff grand slams. On top of it all, his friendly demeanor, tireless work ethic and community involvement made Thome the most popular athlete in Cleveland.

When he became a free agent in 2002, Thome was willing to accept less than his market value to stay in Cleveland. But the team would not grant his request for a six-year contract, and Thome left to join the Phillies, a move that angered many of the Indians' faithful. Philadelphia fans quickly embraced their new first baseman, who blasted 47 taters in 2003 (one shy of Mike Schmidt's franchise record), and 42 more the following season. But he was injured for most of 2005, and his spot at first base was filled by rookie Ryan Howard, whose obvious talent made Thome expendable in Philadelphia.

Thome accepted a trade to Chicago in 2006, pleased to be playing in his home state, and to be back in the American League, where his big frame would not have to patrol the infield. In his first campaign as the White Sox' designated hitter, Thome was named Comeback Player of the Year as he returned to form with another 42-homer season and a trip to his fifth All-Star Game.

On May 29, he returned to Cleveland and was roundly booed by the crowd at Jacobs Field as he walked to the plate for his first at-bat. He answered by pounding a two-run homer to right-center off Cliff Lee. In the sixth, he hit another two-run shot to turn the game into a 10–0 rout.

Comfortable in Chicago, Thome played two more full seasons with the White Sox and tallied a combined 69 homers and 186 RBIs. In late 2009, he had a sojourn with the Los Angeles Dodgers, who used him as a pinch hitter down the stretch and during their brief appearance in the postseason.

A free agent before the 2010 season, the big man decided to play his 20th big-league season with the Minnesota Twins. As a DH and pinch-hitter, he posted good numbers: a .283 average (.302 against right-handers) and an OPS of 1.039, his best mark in eight years. Many of his 25 home runs had historical significance, as Thome continues to inch past the game's all-time great power hitters. On June 19, his pinch-hit homer in the ninth inning was his 570th, moving him past Rafael Palmeiro into 11th place on the all-time list. Later in the year he passed Harmon Killebrew, Mark McGwire and Frank Robinson into the number-eight spot. He also belted his 12th career walk-off home run, tying the all-time record. With 589 career home runs, Jim Thome is edging ever closer to the magic 600.

MARK BUEHRLE - Chicago White Sox

CHRIS CARPENTER - St. Louis Cardinals

ZACK GREINKE - Milwaukee Brewers

ROY HALLADAY - Philadelphia Phillies

FELIX HERNANDEZ - Seattle Mariners

TIM HUDSON - Atlanta Braves

UBALDO JIMENEZ - Colorado Rockies

JOSH JOHNSON - Florida Marlins

CLIFF LEE - Philadelphia Phillies

JON LESTER - Boston Red Sox

TIM LINCECUM - San Francisco Giants

ROY OSWALT - Philadelphia Phillies

DAVID PRICE - Tampa Bay Rays

CC SABATHIA - New York Yankees

JOHAN SANTANA - New York Mets

JUSTIN VERLANDER - Detroit Tigers

ADAM WAINWRIGHT - St. Louis Cardinals

JERED WEAVER - Los Angeles Angels of Anaheim

Armed and
DANGEROUS

mark BUEHRLE

CHICAGO WHITE SOX ◆ AL Central

As pitching prospects go, Mark Buehrle was about as unpromising as they come. He did not even make his high school baseball team until his junior year, and when no major universities came knocking, Buehrle ended up at Jefferson College in his home state of Missouri. A perfect 8–0 record in his freshman season finally caught the scouts' attention. The Chicago White Sox decided to spend a lowly 38th round draft pick on him in 1998 and clearly were not expecting much.

But the young lefty turned out to be a quick study. Buehrle had an average fastball, but also possessed a good slider, a curve and a changeup, and could throw all of them for strikes. The White Sox — who by then had built a 9½-game lead atop the AL Central — were convinced he was for real, and they called him up in July 2000. A major-league pennant race was a high-pressure situation for a pitcher who 12 months earlier had been throwing to Class-A batters. But Buehrle displayed the poise he would soon be renowned for. In 25 relief appearances and three starts he went 4–1. Opponents soon learned one of his trademarks: his deadly pickoff move, which he used to erase any runner who leaned too far toward second. (Since 2001, Buehrle has led the majors with 74 pickoffs.)

At spring training in 2001, Buehrle earned a spot in the starting rotation. After struggling early, he put together a string of 24 scoreless innings and won five straight to turn his season around. He finished at 16–8 with a 3.29 ERA and led the league with a stingy 1.07 WHIP. In 2002, he won 19 games for a mediocre White Sox club and made his first All-Star Team, emerging as one of the finest left-handers in the American League. While he rarely overpowered hitters, Buehrle used his excellent command to get ahead in the count and produce ground-ball outs.

In 2005, the White Sox had the best rotation in the league, with Buehrle (16–8) and Jon Garland (18–10) leading the way. The team won 99 games that year to

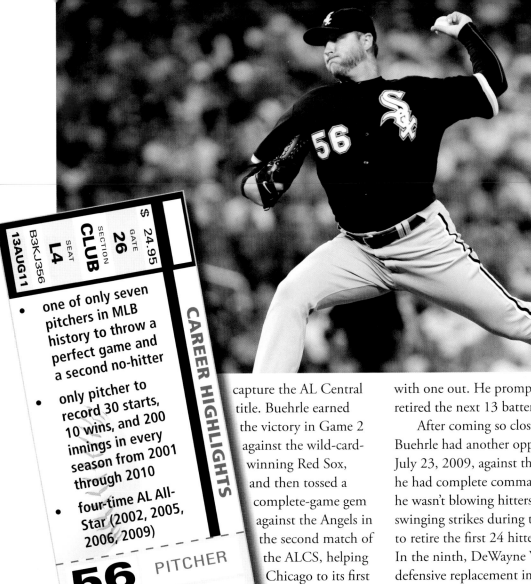

$ 24.95

GATE 26

SECTION CLUB

SEAT L4

B3KJ356

13AUG11

CAREER HIGHLIGHTS

- one of only seven pitchers in MLB history to throw a perfect game and a second no-hitter

- only pitcher to record 30 starts, 10 wins, and 200 innings in every season from 2001 through 2010

- four-time AL All-Star (2002, 2005, 2006, 2009)

56 PITCHER

Mark BUEHRLE

capture the AL Central title. Buehrle earned the victory in Game 2 against the wild-card-winning Red Sox, and then tossed a complete-game gem against the Angels in the second match of the ALCS, helping Chicago to its first pennant since 1959.

In the Fall Classic, Buehrle started Game 2 against the Houston Astros and did not figure in the decision, but he made his contribution — and World Series history — two nights later. Game 3 was a marathon that stretched into the 14th inning before the White Sox finally scored two in the top of the frame. When Houston put two men on in the bottom of the inning, the pivotal match was suddenly in jeopardy. Having already used eight pitchers, the depleted Sox turned to Buehrle, who got Adam Everett to pop up for the final out. It was the first time a pitcher in a World Series had earned a save after starting the previous game, and it stuck a fork in the Astros, who were swept the next day.

The White Sox had a dismal 2007, but Buehrle's third start of the season was one of the few highlights. On April 18 against the Texas Rangers, he took a perfect game into the fifth inning before walking Sammy Sosa

with one out. He promptly picked off Sosa and then retired the next 13 batters for a no-hit masterpiece.

After coming so close to perfection in that game, Buehrle had another opportunity to make history on July 23, 2009, against the Tampa Bay Rays. While he had complete command of his repertoire that day, he wasn't blowing hitters away. He produced only six swinging strikes during the whole match, but managed to retire the first 24 hitters during eight spotless innings. In the ninth, DeWayne Wise entered the game as a defensive replacement in left field. The first Rays batter, Gabe Kapler, promptly belted one over the wall, but Wise made a spectacular leaping grab to steal a home run. Buehrle retired the next two batters to nail down the 18th perfect game in history.

Amazingly, Buehrle's streak continued in his next start against the Minnesota Twins. He set down the first 17 hitters he faced before issuing a walk in the sixth inning. That added up to a string of 45 consecutive batters retired, a new MLB record.

Buehrle won his first Gold Glove Award in 2009 and ensured his second on Opening Day the following season. Cleveland's Lou Marson ripped a pitch up the middle, and Buehrle stuck out his left leg like a goalie and deflected the ball toward foul territory in front of first base. Then the pitcher sprinted off the mound, scooped the ball with his glove and shoveled it through his legs as he tumbled toward the dugout. First baseman Paul Konerko barehanded the toss to nab the runner in a play that many considered one of the greatest they'd ever seen. With Mark Buehrle on the mound, fans have come to expect that kind of perfection.

chris
CARPENTER 29

If you were to look at Chris Carpenter's statistics before and after 2004, you'd never know they belonged to the same pitcher. The right-hander made his debut in 1997 with Toronto and went on to have six dreary and injury-riddled seasons with the Blue Jays, during which he was 49–50 with an ERA near 5.00. Then he was miraculously reborn with the St. Louis Cardinals in 2004. Since joining his new club, Carpenter's record is a glowing 84–33, and he's collected a Cy Young Award and a World Series ring.

By 1999, the Blue Jays hoped their first-round pick would round out a talented young pitching staff that included Kelvim Escobar and a 22-year-old Roy Halladay. But that September Carpenter had a bone spur removed from his right elbow, and his 2000 season was a disaster. Late in 2002, after he suffered a torn labrum in his shoulder, the Blue Jays finally took his name off the 40-man roster and asked him to accept a demotion to the minors. Carpenter refused and became a free agent. Although they knew he would have to sit out the entire 2003 campaign to nurse the shoulder, the Cardinals took a chance and offered him a contract.

Back on the mound in 2004, Carpenter was finally throwing without pain. He was like a completely new pitcher, having regained command of his cutter and curveball, as well as his mid-90s fastball, and in 28 starts he was a stellar 15–5. Carpenter's transformation wasn't purely physical. The six-foot-six righty also changed his mental makeup and took a newfound composure to the mound. He knew the Cardinals took a big chance when they signed him, and he wanted to prove their faith wasn't misplaced.

In 2005, Carpenter was the picture of consistency: from June through early September, he made 22 quality starts in a row and won 13 straight decisions. He became the majors' first 20-game winner in just his 26th start and closed out the regular season with a magnificent 21–5 record, a 2.83 ERA, and a career-high

213 strikeouts. He was a big reason why the Cardinals won 100 games and captured the NL Central again, but this time the club lost the NLCS to the Houston Astros. The following month, Carpenter took home the NL Cy Young Award.

With Carpenter now leading the staff and a lineup that featured Albert Pujols and Scott Rolen, the Cardinals won their third straight division title in 2006. The ace's 3.09 ERA was second best in the National League, but he saved his best stuff for the postseason. Carpenter beat the Padres in the NLDS opener and again in the deciding fourth game before the Mets roughed him up in Game 2 of the Championship Series, which the Cardinals eventually won in seven. That sent St. Louis to the World Series against the Detroit Tigers. The clubs split the first two games, and Carpenter got the ball for the pivotal third match. He tossed an absolute gem: eight shutout innings, allowing three hits. The Cards won 5–0 and then went on to take the next two games and their

first championship since 1982.

Then the injury nightmares returned. Carpenter missed virtually all of the 2007 and 2008 seasons, recovering from Tommy John surgery and more shoulder troubles. But he made another triumphant return in 2009. He didn't allow an earned run in his first four starts (spanning 23 innings), and then won 11 straight decisions from July to early September. His 17–4 record and 2.24 ERA were both tops in the National League, and although he finished a close second to Tim Lincecum in the Cy Young voting, he was named NL Pitcher of the Year by *The Sporting News.*

The Cardinals missed the postseason in 2010, but Carpenter was again one of the league's top hurlers with 16 wins and a 3.22 ERA. Even more impressive were his 35 starts (the most in the majors) and his 235 innings, his highest total since his Cy Young season in 2005. The fact that he can carry a workload like that after so many arm problems proves that this Carpenter has all the right tools.

$ 24.95
GATE
SECTION 41
SEAT CLUB
B5
R3SD167
3JUNE11

CAREER HIGHLIGHTS

- leads all MLB starters with a .718 winning percentage (84–33) since 2004
- only pitcher to win NL Comeback Player of the Year Award twice (2004, 2009)
- three-time NL All-Star (2005, 2006, 2010)

29 PITCHER

Chris **CARPENTER**

zack GREINKE

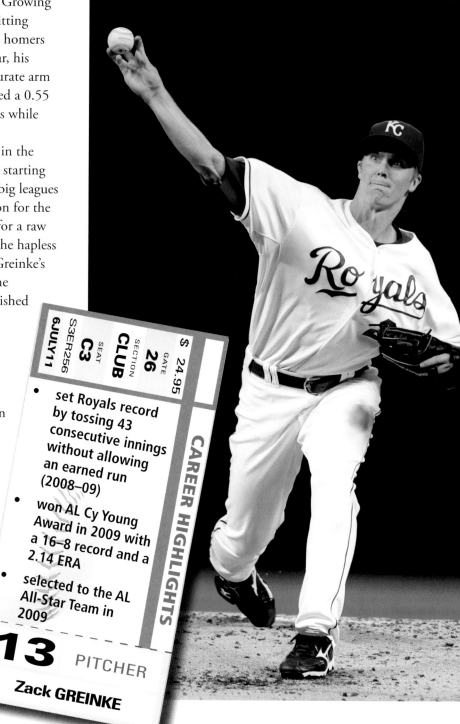

Zack Greinke never wanted to be a pitcher. Growing up in Orlando, Florida, he was a power-hitting shortstop and first baseman who pounded 31 homers in his high school career. But in his senior year, his coaches recognized that his powerful and accurate arm belonged on the mound. That season he posted a 0.55 ERA, and in 63 innings he fanned 118 batters while walking only 8.

The Royals grabbed Greinke sixth overall in the 2002 draft, and when they were desperate for starting pitchers in 2004 they summoned him to the big leagues ahead of schedule. He remained in the rotation for the rest of the season and threw remarkably well for a raw 20-year-old, but he got little assistance from the hapless Royals offense, which averaged 1.36 runs in Greinke's 11 losses. From late July to early September, he managed to win six of seven decisions and finished the year with an 8–11 record and a team-best 3.97 ERA, tops among major-league rookies.

Despite his talents, however, Greinke had difficulty getting along in the clubhouse. He was often aloof, and when he did speak to teammates he could be downright rude. When the Royals chose him as their pitcher of the year in 2004, Greinke went to the awards presentation but openly scoffed that "it didn't mean anything."

Greinke pitched well in his first eight starts of 2005, posting a 3.09 ERA by mid-May, though he was 0–4 due to a complete lack of run support. Then the wheels came off. He got shelled in several starts, and by the All-Star break his ERA was over 6.00. He eventually finished the year with a league-worst 17 losses. The only bright spot came in June, when he homered off Russ Ortiz of Arizona for his first major-league hit.

$ 24.95
GATE 26
SECTION CLUB
SEAT C3
S3ER256
6JULY11

CAREER HIGHLIGHTS

- set Royals record by tossing 43 consecutive innings without allowing an earned run (2008–09)

- won AL Cy Young Award in 2009 with a 16–8 record and a 2.14 ERA

- selected to the AL All-Star Team in 2009

13 PITCHER

Zack GREINKE

Along the way there was more odd behavior. During one bullpen session, he was so filled with rage that he threw nothing but unrestrained fastballs until he broke down in frustration. Before the start of the 2006 season, Greinke finally confessed to the K.C. organization that he was miserable. The pressure of being a major league pitcher was more than he could handle. He told his family that he was through with baseball.

With the club's encouragement, Greinke took several months off and was eventually treated for depression and a social anxiety disorder. He responded well, and was ready to get back on the mound by June 2006. He pitched for three months in Double-A and then returned to the Royals in September, where he made one start and two relief appearances.

He still had some struggles ahead, though. When he opened the 2007 campaign by going 1–4 with a 5.71 ERA in his first seven starts, the Royals moved him to the bullpen. But by August Greinke was back in the rotation and made seven more starts, in which he posted a stellar 1.85 ERA. Then the young righty proved he had put his troubles behind him with a breakout season in 2008: he won 13 games with a 3.47 ERA, both career bests, and the Royals were impressed enough to sign the 24-year-old to a four-year deal.

At spring training in 2009, Greinke worked on adding a new pitch to his repertoire. He already threw a nasty slider, a humming fastball and a paralyzing curve, all with varying speeds and extraordinary control. Now he worked hard to add a changeup, which kept hitters even more off balance.

When the season opened, Greinke was simply unhittable. Over his first four starts, he didn't allow an earned run, and in April and May he was 8–1 with a 1.10 ERA. In late August, he struck out 15 batters en route to his 12th win, then tossed a one-hit shutout in his next start. He won his last five decisions to compile a 16–8 record on a last-place team. He led the American League in ERA (2.14), WHIP (1.073) and was second in strikeouts with 242, while walking only 51. At the end of the season, he scooped his first Cy Young Award.

Greinke followed up his lights-out season with a disappointing 2010. In early June he was a miserable 1–8, though his ERA was below 3.00 for much of that period, as he again suffered from anemic run support. He managed to go 10–6 the rest of the way, though his 4.17 ERA was his highest since 2005. In the offseason, the Royals traded him to the Milwaukee Brewers for a handful of prospects.

Greinke will now have to prove himself on a new club — although the high-school slugger will likely welcome the opportunity to get some at-bats in the National League. Of course, the young pitcher has overcome far more difficult challenges. One of his strengths is his ability to work through difficult situations. Whether it's in a game with men on base, or when battling his personal demons, Zack Greinke knows how to pull out his best stuff when it matters most.

roy HALLADAY 34

Every ballplayer starts the season with a dream of making it to the World Series. But heading into 2010, it would be fair to say that no one wanted it quite as badly as Roy Halladay. Arguably the best pitcher in baseball since 2002, Halladay had spent a dozen seasons with the Toronto Blue Jays without so much as a whiff of the postseason. Then, in December 2009, the Jays dealt Halladay to the Philadelphia Phillies, who were two-time defending NL champs. Suddenly the World Series seemed within his grasp.

"Doc" Halladay grew up in a suburb of Denver and was the Blue Jays' first-round pick in 1995. He broke into the big leagues as a September call-up in 1998, and in his second start, the 21-year-old tossed a near-perfect gem against the Detroit Tigers. Only one batter had reached base before Halladay had his no-hit bid spoiled by a pinch home run with two outs in the ninth.

Halladay's career almost ended in 2000, when his mechanics suddenly broke down. After winning his first start, he was pounded in the next six, and by late July his ERA was a bloated 11.05. He eventually found himself all the way back in Class-A, where he rebuilt his delivery and changed his approach, as he came to realize that he didn't have to blow away every hitter. He learned to keep the ball down to induce grounders, and he mastered the cut fastball that would become his deadliest weapon. Halladay was transformed, and in 2002 he posted a 19–7 record and a 2.93 ERA, fifth best in the American League.

Halladay's 2003 season was among the best ever posted by a Toronto starter. He went 15–0 from May through July, and in September, he tossed the majors' first 10-inning shutout in 13 years, blanking the Tigers 1–0 during a streak of 23 consecutive scoreless frames. He ended up with a league-leading 22 wins against 7 losses, a 3.25 ERA and 204 strikeouts against just 32 bases on balls. He was an easy choice for the AL Cy Young Award.

CAREER HIGHLIGHTS

- leads all active pitchers in complete games (58), shutouts (19) and winning percentage (.663, minimum 1,000 innings pitched)

- one of only five pitchers to have won the Cy Young Award in both leagues

- selected to seven All-Star Teams between 2002 and 2010

34 PITCHER

Roy HALLADAY

After an injury riddled 2004, Halladay spent five more outstanding seasons in Toronto. He was a combined 44–16 from 2005 through 2007 as he further adjusted his repertoire, adding a changeup and throwing more sinkers to encourage ground balls and avoid the arm fatigue that used to hamper him late in the year. In 2008, he reached the 20-win milestone for the second time, while posting a 2.48 ERA and a major-league leading WHIP of 1.053. He won 17 more in 2009 and had a career-high 208 strikeouts.

When the Phillies acquired Doc before the 2010 season, everyone had high expectations — some even speculated that he could win 30 games. While he fell well short of that impossible goal, Halladay's season was magical. He went the distance three times in his first seven starts (two of them shutouts) and was 6–1 with a 1.45 ERA in mid-May. Then he lost his next two decisions before going to the mound on May 29 against the Florida Marlins. He mowed down batter after batter with pinpoint control, and just as he did way back in 1998, Doc went to the ninth inning without having allowed a hit or a walk. The Marlins sent three pinch hitters to the plate, and this time Halladay disposed of all of them to complete the 20th perfect game in MLB history.

Halladay went on to win his first four starts in September, and the Phillies had a chance to clinch the NL East in his last game. With his sights on the postseason, Doc was magnificent again. He needed just 97 pitches to blank the Washington Nationals with a two-hit shutout to seal the Phillies fourth straight division title.

When he went to the hill for Game 1 against Cincinnati in the NLDS, Halladay had a dozen years of pent-up playoff drive bubbling inside him. The Reds were the best hitting team in the National League that season, but they were no match for Doc at the top of his game. He was perfect until he walked Jay Bruce in the fifth, and then set down the next 13 for a no-hitter — the only playoff no-no since Don Larsen's perfect game in the 1956 World Series. The shell-shocked Reds rolled over and were swept in three straight.

Although Doc beat Tim Lincecum in Game 5 of the NLCS to stave off elimination, the Giants won the next match and ended the Phillies season. Halladay was the unanimous winner of the Cy Young Award with his league-leading 21 wins, a 2.44 ERA, 250 innings pitched, 9 complete games, and a personal-best 218 strikeouts. He fell short of his goal of a championship ring, but having accomplished everything else in 2010, Doc needs something to reach for in the seasons to come.

felix
HERNANDEZ 34

Major-league scouts see a lot of young fireballers who will never amount to anything. When the Seattle Mariners watched a teenaged Felix Hernandez, however, they recognized that he was something special — a child prodigy. Born in 1986 in Valencia, Venezuela, Hernandez could throw over 90 miles per hour when he was 14 years old. But players aren't eligible for the draft until at least age 16, so the Mariners had to wait until 2002 to grab him.

The year he turned 18, Hernandez went 14–4 in the minors, and when he dominated at Triple-A the next season, the Mariners felt he was ready for the big time. When he made his MLB debut in August 2005, Hernandez was 19 years, 118 days old, the youngest starting pitcher in more than 20 seasons. The right-hander showed a poise and maturity that belied his age. In his second game, he tossed eight scoreless frames against the Twins to get his first win. He didn't allow an extra-base hit until his fifth start, a span of 112 batters, and lasted at least seven innings in 10 of his 12 starts that year, posting an ERA of 2.67.

"King Felix," as he was nicknamed, was still a teenager as the 2006 season kicked off. (The Mariners pitching staff also included the league's oldest player: Jamie Moyer, 43, made his big-league debut two months after Hernandez was born.) Hernandez was inconsistent that season, but showed flashes of brilliance, including a five-hit shutout against the Los Angeles Angels. He finished the year 12–14, but even that was enough to lead the weak Mariners staff in wins.

In his second start of 2007, Hernandez was pitted against Boston's Daisuke Matsuzaka, who had been the biggest pitching story of the offseason. The Japanese legend had won his MLB debut five days earlier with a 10-strikeout performance on the road, and his first start at Fenway had all the hype you'd expect from the Boston media. But it was Hernandez who stole the

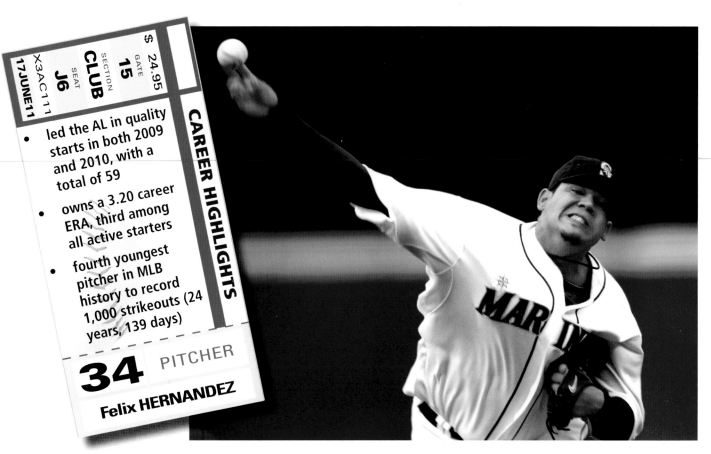

CAREER HIGHLIGHTS

- led the AL in quality starts in both 2009 and 2010, with a total of 59

- owns a 3.20 career ERA, third among all active starters

- fourth youngest pitcher in MLB history to record 1,000 strikeouts (24 years, 139 days)

34 PITCHER

Felix HERNANDEZ

headlines: he took a no-hitter into the eighth and wound up allowing one harmless single as he blanked the Red Sox 3–0. He went on to post a 14–7 record that season with a 3.92 ERA, the lowest in the Seattle rotation.

After a strong start in 2008, Hernandez faltered in May, but then won his first three starts in June before the Mariners rolled into Shea Stadium to face the Mets. The opening game of the series was a much-anticipated matchup between Hernandez and his fellow Venezuelan, Johan Santana. After the two aces traded scoreless frames, Santana allowed two hits in the second before a fielding error loaded the bases, bringing Hernandez to the plate. Santana tried to get ahead with a fastball, but King Felix sent it over the wall in right-center for an improbable grand slam — the first ever by a pitcher in interleague play.

Although 2009 was his fifth in the big leagues, Hernandez was still only 23, and it was clear that he was nowhere close to reaching his potential. That was about to change. He won his first four decisions, but then he stumbled in May and got rocked in three of his starts. That was the turning point, however. He was a perfect 3–0 with a 0.94 ERA in June, and was finally rewarded with his first All-Star selection that July. After the break he piled up 10 wins to finish the season at 19-5, with a 2.49 ERA and 217 strikeouts.

Heading into 2010, the talk of Seattle was Cliff Lee, the former Cy Young winner who joined the Mariners in the offseason. But it was Hernandez who proved to be the American League's best starter that year, despite toiling for its worst team. He led the AL with 249 innings pitched (the most in the AL in seven years), struck out 232 batters (one shy of the league lead), and his 2.27 ERA was the stingiest in the majors and set a franchise record.

Unfortunately, the King got no help from his subjects. Despite leading the majors with 30 quality starts in 34 tries, he was charged with 12 losses on the year. In those dozen defeats, his teammates scored a grand total of seven runs while he was on the mound. Over his final 10 starts, he allowed eight earned runs for a 0.96 ERA — and lost three times. After the season, the baseball media debated whether you could hand the Cy Young Award to a pitcher with only 13 wins. But justice prevailed and Hernandez received 21 of 28 first-place votes to edge out David Price (19–6) and CC Sabathia (21–7).

The Mariners have handled their young superstar well over the years, limiting his workload and shutting him down at the first sign of soreness. They've been rewarded with a durable and dangerous arm that may get even better. Still in his mid-20s, this King looks like he'll reign for many more years.

tim HUDSON

15

Tim Hudson is a southern gentleman through and through, but put him on a pitcher's mound and he becomes a bulldog.

Hudson grew up in Columbus, Georgia, where his idols were the great Atlanta Braves pitchers of the 1990s: John Smoltz, Steve Avery, Tom Glavine and Greg Maddux. He was a small, skinny kid who was constantly underestimated. Although he was a fine athlete in high school, he was under six feet and weighed barely 150 pounds, which was enough to turn off every college and major-league scout in the country. He eventually got an offer from Auburn, who could see that Hudson's grit and determination more than made up for his size. During his two years at Auburn he learned to throw the split-finger fastball that would eventually become his signature pitch. He would later add a changeup and a filthy slider to go along with it.

Hudson made his debut with the Oakland A's in 1999, and struck out 11 batters over five innings. His most memorable start came at Fenway Park when the rookie outpitched Pedro Martinez in a 6–2 Oakland win. His breakout season came the following year, when the 24-year-old went 20–6 and helped the A's to a division title. Down the stretch, he won all of his last seven starts with a 1.16 ERA, the final victory coming on the last day of the season to clinch a playoff berth.

During his six seasons in Oakland, the righty was 92–39 (.702) with a 3.30 ERA. The trio of Hudson, Barry Zito and Mark Mulder was the core of an outstanding young pitching staff that led the Athletics to the postseason four straight years. Hudson's best season came in 2003, when he posted a 2.70 ERA and a WHIP of 1.075, both career bests. His 16–7 record should have been even better, but Oakland's closer Keith Foulke, who blew only five saves all year, unfortunately had four that were in Hudson's starts.

Hudson was set to become a free agent after the 2005 season. The A's knew they would be outbid when

he looked for a new contract, so they traded him to the Atlanta Braves for three prospects. Hudson had loved playing in Oakland, but now he relished the idea of pitching in his home state alongside John Smoltz, one of his childhood idols.

In his first year in Atlanta, Hudson and Smoltz each won 14 games to lead the club to its 14th consecutive division title. Hudson lost his start in Game 1 of the 2005 NLDS against Houston, but the Braves went to their ace again in Game 4, and this time he pitched into the eighth inning before leaving with a 6–1 lead. Then the bullpen imploded: the Astros' Lance Berkman hit a grand slam, and Brad Ausmus homered with two outs in the ninth to tie it. The game turned out to be the longest in playoff history. The 18-inning marathon finally ended when Houston rookie Chris Burke clinched the series with a walk-off home run.

Following a disappointing 2006 campaign, Hudson bounced back the next year with 16 wins and a 3.33 ERA, his best in four seasons. He was even better in the first half of 2008, as he collected nine wins before the All-Star break while sharing the rotation with another of his heroes: 42-year-old Tom Glavine returned to the Braves that year to close out his Hall of Fame career. In July, however, Hudson learned he would need Tommy John surgery, which would put him on the shelf for at least a year.

No one was surprised when the skinny kid from Columbus, Georgia, returned with renewed strength. Hudson's 2010 season was his best in seven years: he went 17–9 with a 2.83 ERA and a 1.15 WHIP as he led the Braves back to the playoffs for the first time since 2005. Hudson was brilliant in his Game 3 start in the NLDS, an epic pitchers' duel against San Francisco's Jonathan Sanchez. Hudson allowed just one unearned run over seven innings, while Sanchez had a no-hitter going in the sixth before

Hudson broke it up with a solid single. The Braves went to the ninth with a 2–1 lead, but the Giants rallied and ended up taking the series in four games. For the sixth time in a dozen seasons, Hudson's team bowed out of the postseason in the first round and denied him the opportunity to play for a pennant.

$ 24.95
GATE 23
SECTION UPPER
SEAT T44
E1FH536
15JULY11

CAREER HIGHLIGHTS

- has never had a losing record in 12 major-league seasons (1999–2010)
- named NL Comeback Player of the Year in 2010
- three-time All-Star (2000, 2004, 2010)

15   PITCHER

Tim HUDSON

ubaldo JIMENEZ

38

COLORADO ROCKIES ◆ NL West

When Ubaldo Jimenez was 17, the Rockies organization sent some scouts to have a look at his repertoire. Everyone knew the kid could throw hard — he would later develop what may be the liveliest fastball in the majors, occasionally touching 100 miles per hour. What they weren't expecting was the way he could make a baseball dance. The first time Ubaldo threw his curveball, it broke so sharply that it struck the catcher in the neck.

Jimenez became a regular in the Colorado rotation after the All-Star break in 2007, and that August he strung together three starts during which he allowed only two earned runs over 20 innings. The Rockies won 14 of their last 15 games down the stretch, and on the last day of the regular schedule they needed a win to force a one-game playoff against the Padres for the NL wild card. With everything on the line, they went to

their rookie fireballer, and he allowed just one hit while striking out 10 before leaving in the seventh with a 1–0 lead. The Rockies went on to win that game and the tiebreaker to earn a berth in the postseason.

Colorado won both of Jimenez's playoff starts against the Phillies and Diamondbacks, storming into the World Series, where their magical season was snuffed out by the Boston Red Sox. When Jimenez went to the mound in Game 2 of the Fall Classic to try to even the series against Curt Schilling, he left in the fifth trailing just 2–1, but the Rockies could not score another run. They lost the game and were ousted by the Bosox in four straight.

In his first full season in the majors in 2008, Jimenez was already a miserable 1–7 with an ERA of 4.85 in June when he went to the mound against his countryman and boyhood idol, Pedro Martinez. In one of his best outings of the year, he held the Mets to one run in a 7–1 Rockies

$ 24.95

GATE 29

SECTION CLUB

SEAT M5

B2SR668

1SEPT11

CAREER HIGHLIGHTS

- has held batters to a .227 average over his career despite playing in one of the most hitter-friendly parks in baseball

- tossed the only no-hitter in Rockies' history on April 17, 2010

- chosen as the NL's starting pitcher in the 2010 All-Star Game

38 PITCHER

Ubaldo JIMENEZ

victory that proved to be the turning point in his season. Jimenez went 8–3 in the second half as he finally gained command of all his pitches: curveball, two-seamer, slider, changeup and, of course, his explosive fastball.

The 2009 World Baseball Classic was a sneak preview of what Jimenez had in store for the next two seasons. He started for the Dominican Republic in an early-round game against the Netherlands and struck out 10 of the 13 flailing Dutchmen he faced. When the regular season kicked off, he started slowly, but then rebounded with another strong second half and was 9–3 after the break. The Rockies had been 15 games behind in early June, but they roared back to take the NL wild card with 92 wins, and Jimenez had earned the role of Game 1 starter. Cliff Lee and the Phillies outmatched him in the NLDS opener, but in their Game 4 rematch Jimenez allowed two runs over seven innings (both solo homers) and the Rockies took a 4–2 lead into the ninth. It didn't last: the Phillies rallied against closer Huston Street and won the deciding game 5–4.

Jimenez's performance in the first half of 2010 was otherworldly. After winning his first two starts, he went to the hill against Atlanta on April 17 with electric stuff.

He walked six, but thanks to a pickoff, a double play and a spectacular diving catch by center fielder Dexter Fowler, Jimenez got to the ninth without allowing a hit. He got two quick outs on a popup and a short fly ball to bring up catcher Brian McCann. Jimenez came inside with a high fastball, and McCann grounded out weakly to second to give Jimenez the first no-hitter in franchise history.

He followed his no-no with two more scoreless outings, then hurled 33 consecutive scoreless frames in late May and early June. In his first 11 starts, Jimenez was 10–1 and his ERA was a microscopic 0.78. He notched his 15th win before the break — the first player to accomplish that feat since 1988 — and was named the starting pitcher for the NL All-Star Team. Jimenez was a disappointing 4–7 in the second half of 2010, but he still had a chance to reach 20 wins in his final start of the season against the Cardinals. He was utterly dominating, twirling eight shutout frames and striking out 10, but the Rockies came up empty and lost 1–0 in 11 innings. Jimenez finished his best season to date at 19–8 with a 2.88 ERA and 214 strikeouts.

Jimenez's success rests in his ability to keep the ball down: when he has his best stuff, he can tail the ball away from both left- and right-handed hitters, forcing them to hit ground balls. At homer-happy Coors Field, that's essential to a pitcher's survival, and no one does it better than Ubaldo Jimenez.

josh
JOHNSON

FLORIDA MARLINS ◆ NL East

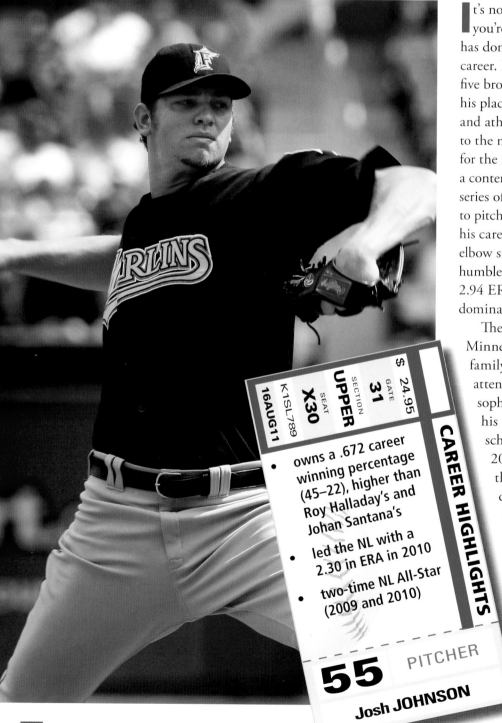

It's not easy to keep a low profile when you're six-foot-seven, but Josh Johnson has done that for much of his baseball career. He grew up as the youngest of five brothers who liked to keep him in his place, even though he was as talented and athletic as any of them. Since getting to the major leagues, Johnson has toiled for the Marlins, a team that hasn't been a contender for years, and he's battled a series of injuries that have allowed him to pitch only one uninterrupted season in his career. But since coming back from elbow surgery in mid-2008, the quiet, humble fastballer has gone 33–12 with a 2.94 ERA, making him one of the most dominating starting pitchers in the game.

The big right-hander was born in Minnesota, but when he was five his family moved to Tulsa, Oklahoma. Josh attended Jenks High School, and as a sophomore he shared the outfield with his older brother, Tyler, when the school won a state championship in 2000. During one game that year, the 16-year-old right fielder gunned down a runner at home with a bullet-like throw, and it was clear that this kid had a special arm. They turned him into a pitcher, and in his senior year Johnson led Jenks to a second state title in 2002. The Marlins drafted him that same year.

Johnson started his 2006 rookie season in the bullpen, but quickly earned a spot in the starting

Ticket / Career Highlights card

$ 24.95

GATE **31**

SECTION **UPPER**

SEAT **X30**

K1SL789

16AUG11

CAREER HIGHLIGHTS

- owns a .672 career winning percentage (45–22), higher than Roy Halladay's and Johan Santana's
- led the NL with a 2.30 in ERA in 2010
- two-time NL All-Star (2009 and 2010)

55 PITCHER

Josh JOHNSON

rotation. Using his lively fastball, power slider, and an occasional changeup, he went 11–5 with a 3.03 ERA in his 24 starts that season. During one five-game span in May and June, he started against Pedro Martinez, Roy Halladay and John Smoltz and beat all three Cy Young winners, posting an ERA of 1.38 over that stretch. By the end of July, he was leading the National League in ERA. But with a couple of weeks to go, Johnson complained of soreness in his right forearm and didn't start again after September 12.

When the arm didn't respond to treatment during the offseason, Johnson started the 2007 campaign on the DL and tried to return that June. He made four starts, but after going 0–3 with a 7.47 ERA it was obvious that he would need to go under the knife. He had Tommy John surgery in August and was expected to miss all of 2008. But Johnson wasn't content to keep to that recovery schedule. He worked tirelessly on his rehab and used his time off to study a lot of videos, as he prepared himself for his return to the mound. He was back in the Marlins lineup in July 2008, just 11 months after the surgery, and went 7–1 in 14 starts that season.

As the 2009 season opened, Johnson looked forward to finally spending a full schedule in the Marlins rotation. With his arm troubles behind him, he bolted out of the gate with 14 scoreless innings in his first two starts, and by late June he was 7–1 with a 2.66 ERA, good enough for a spot on his first All-Star Team. On August 14 he took a no-hitter into the

seventh inning and struck out 11 to run his record to 12–2. When the season was done, Johnson was 15–5 (the second-best winning percentage in the NL) with a 3.23 ERA. Most encouragingly, he hurled over 200 innings for the first time in his career.

The baseball media were buzzing in the first half of 2010, which saw perfect games by Roy Halladay and Dallas Braden, and a 15–1 streak by Ubaldo Jimenez, which included a no-hitter. But through it all, Josh Johnson may have been the best of that bunch. The Marlins ace sported a 1.62 ERA after 19 outings, and he became the first pitcher since 1995 to have a run of 13 starts without allowing more than two runs. Although Jimenez got the start in the All-Star Game, Johnson pitched two perfect innings, striking out Ichiro Suzuki and Derek Jeter as the National League won its first Midsummer Classic since 1996.

In August, however, Johnson strained a muscle in his back and when it didn't improve by September, the Marlins shut him down to be safe. His final numbers included a 2.30 ERA, tops in the National League, but only 11 wins. Seven times during the season, Johnson left the game with the lead only to watch the Marlins bullpen blow it.

While the Marlins' low payroll has prevented them from retaining other talented arms (Josh Beckett, A.J. Burnett, Carl Pavano), the club signed Johnson to a four-year, $39 million contract that will keep him on the mound in Florida until 2013.

cliff LEE

PHILADELPHIA PHILLIES ◆ NL East

On July 26, 2007, Cliff Lee was booed off the field in Cleveland. He had just surrendered seven runs for the third start in a row, and Indians fans had seen enough. Their club was on its way to its first playoff appearance in six years, and Lee wasn't going to be a part of it: he was demoted to Triple-A after the game and would not make another start that season. At that low point in Cliff Lee's career, it would have been impossible to predict that the next 30 months would bring him a Cy Young Award and two legendary trips to the postseason.

Drafted by the Montreal Expos in 2000, Lee was dealt to Cleveland two years later. His breakout season came in 2005, when he amassed 18 wins against only 5 losses. But he was mediocre the following season, and in 2007 everything seemed to fall apart. After his trip to the minors, Lee returned that September to make four relief appearances, but when Cleveland won the AL Central, they didn't put Lee's name on the postseason roster.

In the offseason, Lee changed his mental approach and was reborn in 2008. Spotting his four-seam, two-seam and cut fastballs and a changeup, he kept hitters off balance and mastered his control so completely that he averaged 1.4 walks per nine innings, the lowest rate in the majors. He allowed a total of 11 hits and 1 run in his first four starts, and was 6–0 in early May. By the All-Star break he was 12–2 with a 2.31 ERA, and AL manager Terry Francona picked him to start in the Midsummer Classic. He was a perfect 5–0 in August (with a 1.86 ERA for the month), and won three more games in September to finish with a magnificent 22–3 record and a league-leading 2.54 ERA. He received 24 of 28 first-place votes for the Cy Young Award.

Midway through the 2009 campaign the Indians sent Lee to the Phillies, who were walking away with the NL East. He won seven games for Philadelphia over the final two months and earned the job of

CAREER HIGHLIGHTS

- winner of the 2008 AL Cy Young Award
- owns a 7–2 record and 2.13 ERA in the postseason (2009–10)
- recorded 185 K's against only 18 bases on balls in 2010, the second-best ratio in MLB history (10.28 strikeouts per walk)

33 | PITCHER

Cliff LEE

Game 1 starter in his first postseason. Lee twirled a complete game to beat Ubaldo Jimenez and the Rockies (he lost his shutout with two outs in the ninth), and allowed just one run in his Game 4 start, which the Phils won in the ninth. Facing the Dodgers in the NLCS, all Lee did was pitch eight shutout innings, striking out 10 in an 11–0 Phillies rout.

Lee saved his best performance for Game 1 of the World Series against the Yankees. Squaring off with his good friend and former teammate CC Sabathia, Lee went the distance, allowing six hits, no walks and fanning 10. The only blemish was a meaningless unearned run in the ninth as the Phillies won 6–1. When Lee returned for Game 5, the Yanks tagged him for five runs, but he still got the victory in an 8–6 win. While the Yankees clinched the series in the next game, Lee wound up 4–0 with a 1.56 ERA in his five postseason starts.

In the offseason, the Phillies decided not to pursue a contract with Lee and instead acquired Roy Halladay in a trade with Toronto. Lee signed a one-year deal with the Seattle Mariners, but at the deadline the M's sent him to the Texas Rangers, who won the AL West virtually uncontested in 2010. That gave Lee another October opportunity.

In two starts against the Tampa Bay Rays in the ALDS, Lee allowed a single run each time and went the distance in the deciding Game 5, when he allowed 6 hits, no walks and struck out 11. He faced the Yanks again in the Championship series, this time going up against Andy Pettitte in Game 3, and baseball's toughest batting order was helpless: Lee allowed two hits over eight shutout innings and punched out 14 batters. He was ready to go for Game 7, but Texas finished off New York in six to advance to the World Series for the first time in franchise history.

Lee finally showed he was mortal in the 2010 Fall Classic. The lefty allowed seven runs before exiting Game 1 in the fifth, and San Francisco won an 11–7 slugfest. With the Rangers facing elimination in Game 5, Lee and Giants ace Tim Lincecum both held their opponents scoreless through six. But in the seventh, series MVP Edgar Renteria popped a three-run homer for the Giants that would stand up as the winner.

The Rangers and Yankees both courted Lee after the 2010 season, but he shocked everyone by announcing he would return to the Phillies — for far less than Texas and New York had offered. After two near-misses in the World Series, it's clear that Cliff Lee's eye is not on money, but on a championship ring.

jon LESTER

Jon Lester learned his signature pitch while toiling with the Portland Sea Dogs in the Double-A Eastern League. It was 2005, and the 21-year-old lefty was already having success with a mid-90s fastball, a slider, a changeup and a curve. Now he added a devastating cutter that could saw off right-handed hitters. That season he went 11–6 with a 2.61 ERA and mowed down 163 batters — more than one per inning.

When the Red Sox found themselves crippled by injuries the following June, they called up the Tacoma native to get a closer look. Lester labored in his major-league debut and escaped with a no-decision, but he was brilliant in his next seven starts and chalked up a perfect 5–0 record. Then he was sidelined in August with back pain that he thought was a result of a minor car accident, but the medical tests came back with shocking results. Lester was diagnosed with a form of blood cancer. Fortunately, it was treatable. He started chemotherapy immediately and was declared fit for spring training the following year. After rehabbing in the minors, Lester made an emotional Fenway homecoming on August 14, 2007, when he allowed just two hits over seven innings in a 2–1 Red Sox win.

The Red Sox finished the 2007 season atop the AL East and knocked off the Angels and the Indians to advance to the Fall Classic. Boston then won the first three games against the Colorado Rockies and was looking for a sweep at Coors

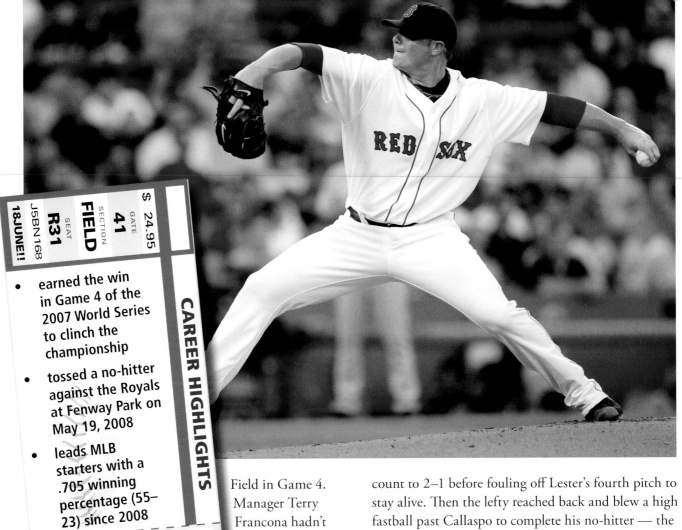

CAREER HIGHLIGHTS

- earned the win in Game 4 of the 2007 World Series to clinch the championship

- tossed a no-hitter against the Royals at Fenway Park on May 19, 2008

- leads MLB starters with a .705 winning percentage (55–23) since 2008

31 PITCHER

Jon LESTER

Field in Game 4. Manager Terry Francona hadn't started Lester in the postseason to that point, but he decided to hand the ball to his young southpaw. The 23-year-old — less than a year after beating cancer — suddenly found himself on the mound in a World Series in front of 50,000 screaming Rockies fans. All he did was toss 5 ²/₃ innings of scoreless ball, allowing just three hits before leaving with the Red Sox ahead 2–0. The bullpen held on for a 4–3 victory and Boston's second championship ring in four years.

Having earned a spot in the rotation for 2008, Lester was inconsistent in the early going. He'd have three or four mediocre starts and then shoot the lights out in his next appearance, and by mid-May he was 2–2 with an ERA near 4.00. In his 11th start he took the mound for an afternoon game at Fenway against the light-hitting Kansas City Royals. He walked a batter in the second, and then mowed down 20 in a row. In the ninth, Esteban German drew a leadoff walk and advanced to third on two weak groundouts. That brought up pinch-hitter Alberto Callaspo, who ran the count to 2–1 before fouling off Lester's fourth pitch to stay alive. Then the lefty reached back and blew a high fastball past Callaspo to complete his no-hitter — the first by a left-handed Red Sox hurler since 1954.

Lester finished 2008 with a 16–6 record and a 3.21 ERA. When the Sox won the wild card, he was outstanding in the ALDS. He won the opener against the Angels (seven innings, one unearned run) and threw seven scoreless frames in Game 4, which the Red Sox won on a walk-off hit in the ninth. He pitched well in both of his starts in the Championship Series, too, but the Tampa Bay pitchers shut down the Boston offense and the Rays took the series in seven games.

When Lester followed with a 15–8 campaign in 2009 — including 225 strikeouts, tops among AL left-handers — he combined with Josh Beckett to give the Red Sox one of the deadliest one-two punches in the league.

In 2010, Lester finally earned a trip to his first All-Star Game after going 11–3 with a 2.78 ERA in the first half. He collected a career-high 19 wins on the year, behind only CC Sabathia in the American League. He's also proven to be one of the game's workhorses: from 2008 through 2010, he's made at least 32 starts and thrown over 200 innings in each season. On the mound and off the field, Jon Lester is a survivor.

tim LINCECUM

SAN FRANCISCO GIANTS ◆ NL West

Tim Lincecum's boyish face, toothy grin and 170-pound frame are anything but intimidating. But when the young righty goes into his windup and unleashes his high-90s fastball or his knee-bending curve, no one is scarier than the guy they call "The Freak."

When Lincecum entered Liberty High School in Renton, Washington, he stood under five feet tall and weighed 85 pounds. He was strong and athletic, however, and his dad helped him engineer a pitching delivery that could squeeze every ounce of power from that tiny body. Tim generated maximum torque by twisting his body and finishing with a huge, lunging step toward the plate. With those unorthodox mechanics, he led Liberty to a state championship.

Lincecum was drafted out of high school by the Chicago Cubs in 2003, but opted to attend the University of Washington, where he won the Golden Spikes Award as the top amateur player of 2006. *Baseball America* ranked both his fastball and his curveball as the best of any college pitcher. Yet when he was eligible for the draft again, most clubs were turned off by his small stature and his crazy mechanics. Nine teams passed him over before the Giants selected him, and their faith in The Freak paid off quickly. Lincecum's minor-league career lasted 13 games, during which he went 6–0, allowed seven earned runs and struck out 104 in 62 innings. He was on the major-league roster 11 months after being drafted, and in his first season with the Giants he went 7–5 with an even 4.00 ERA and 150 K's.

San Francisco was the second-lowest scoring team in the majors in 2008, which makes Lincecum's achievements that year all the more amazing. By mid-June, he was 8–1 with an ERA south of 2.00, even as the Giants were well under .500. In the second half, he went 7–3 and held opposing hitters to a .194 average. He finished the season at 18–5 and his 265 strikeouts were just two shy of the franchise record set by Hall of Famer Christy Mathewson 105 years earlier. He easily won

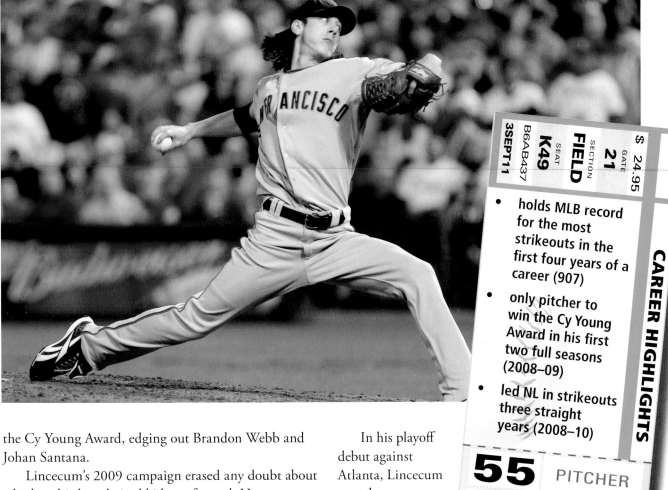

the Cy Young Award, edging out Brandon Webb and Johan Santana.

Lincecum's 2009 campaign erased any doubt about whether this long-haired kid was for real. He was a spectacular 10–2 in the first half, including a string of 29 consecutive scoreless innings, which ended after Lincecum took a no-hitter into the seventh inning before surrendering three straight singles. His second-half ERA was 2.67 and batters were .195 against him, but he won just five more games and finished the year at 15–7. His 2.48 ERA was second best in the NL, and he led the loop with 261 strikeouts, averaging 10.4 per nine innings. In the Cy Young voting that November, Adam Wainwright received more first-place votes, but Lincecum garnered the highest point total and walked off with the award for the second straight year.

Lincecum went 5–0 to open the 2010 season, and the Giants finally had some bats to support him, including newcomers Aubrey Huff, Buster Posey, and later Cody Ross and Pat Burrell. At the beginning of August, they were just 1½ games behind the San Diego Padres in the NL West, but then they stumbled badly. Lincecum lost all five of his starts that month, and by August 25 the club had fallen to 6½ games back. Then it was the Padres turn to go into freefall: they lost 10 straight, while the Giants went 18–8 in September, paced by Lincecum, who was 5–1. The Giants clinched the division in the final game and headed to the postseason for the first time in seven years.

In his playoff debut against Atlanta, Lincecum was almost untouchable. He tossed a two-hit shutout and struck out 14 in a 1–0 gem. He was so dominant that Braves hitters swung through his pitches 28 times. (By comparison, Roy Halladay had thrown 19 swinging strikes in his no-hitter the previous day.) When the Giants faced off against the Phillies in the Championship Series, Lincecum outdueled Halladay in Game 1, and though he lost his Game 5 start, the Giants eventually prevailed in six matches to set up an unlikely World Series against the Texas Rangers.

Game 1 of the Fall Classic was another battle between Cy Young hurlers as Lincecum faced lefty Cliff Lee. But instead of a pitchers' duel, this one ended up being an 11–7 slugfest, with the Giants coming out on top. The two aces met again in Game 5 with San Francisco looking to finish it off, and this time both pitchers were brilliant. Lincecum tossed eight innings, struck out 10 and allowed just three hits. Edgar Renteria's three-run homer was all the Giants needed for a 3–1 win. In his first postseason, Lincecum was 4–1 with a 2.43 ERA and 43 strikeouts, and the Giants were World Series champs for the first time since moving to San Francisco.

roy
OSWALT

44

Roy Oswalt is proof that scouts sometimes need to look in remote places to find exceptional talent. Oswalt grew up in tiny Weir, Mississippi, a town of a few hundred people, where he spent summers helping out on his grandfather's watermelon farm. His high school didn't even have a baseball team until Oswalt's father nagged them into forming one. By 1996, while the diminutive righty was attending a community college near his hometown, hardly anyone even knew about him — except for a trio of scouts with the Houston Astros who encouraged the club to take a flyer with their 23rd-round pick.

Oswalt went 13–4 in Class-A in 1999, but by the end of the season his shoulder was in terrible pain, and he was considering surgery when something bizarre happened. While working under the hood of his truck, Oswalt touched a live wire and got a powerful shock that knocked him senseless. When he came to, the pain in his shoulder was gone — forever. Some have guessed that the shock may have loosened built-up scar tissue, but to the Astros, it must have seemed like divine intervention.

Oswalt debuted with Houston in May 2001, and by June he had won a spot in the rotation. His rookie season was one of the best in years: 14–3 with a 1.06 WHIP, 144 strikeouts and only 24 walks. While the right-hander had a mid-90s fastball, he also threw two different curveballs, one of which was so achingly slow that it had batters lunging as they hit weak grounders.

Before the 2004 season, the Astros went out and

acquired Roger Clemens and Andy Pettitte from the Yankees, assembling a lethal rotation. Clemens took home the Cy Young that year, but it was Oswalt who won 20 games, including 12 in the second half as Houston went from last place on July 24 to a wild card berth.

Then, with Oswalt, Pettitte and Clemens throwing brilliantly all season in 2005, Houston posted the second-lowest ERA in the league. Of their 89 victories, 20 belonged to Oswalt, who was the only pitcher in the majors to rack up back-to-back 20-win campaigns. The Astros repeated as wild-card winners, and Oswalt stepped it up in the playoffs. Facing the Cardinals in the NLCS, he tossed seven innings of one-run ball to win Game 2, then returned in Game 6 and held the Redbirds to three hits, sending Houston to the World Series for the first time in franchise history. In his only start of the Fall Classic in Game 3, however, he was touched for five runs in the fifth and the Chicago White Sox went on to win 7–5 in a 14-inning marathon, completing the sweep the following day.

The Astros ace won a combined 29 games in 2006 and 2007, but he got off to a rough start the following season. By mid-June, his ERA was over 5.00, but then he found his groove. Despite a short stint on the DL, he went 13–5 with a 2.29 ERA the rest of the way and set an Astros team record with 32 ⅓ scoreless innings from August 27 through September 11, including a one-hitter and a three-hitter. He racked up 17 wins in 2008, his highest total in three seasons.

Oswalt mastered a new pitch during the 2010 campaign — a so-called "Vulcan changeup," which is similar to a forkball, but with the ball inserted between the middle and ring fingers. With this new arrow in his quiver, he began the season by throwing 10 consecutive quality starts, but the light-hitting Astros gave him very little run support and he was 3–6 over that span. The pattern continued to the end of July, when the Phillies acquired

CAREER HIGHLIGHTS

- ranks second among all active starters with a career 3.15 ERA
- leads all NL pitchers with 150 wins since 2001
- selected to three consecutive NL All-Star Teams (2005–07)

$ 24.95
GATE 32
SECTION CLUB
SEAT B2
A2DR643
26AUG11

44 PITCHER

Roy OSWALT

him in a trade for J.A. Happ. Oswalt made an immediate and dramatic impact on his new team. The Phils won all of his first 11 starts, and after the trade he had the lowest ERA in the National League (1.74), helping the Phillies nail down the division crown.

With a postseason reputation to live up to, Oswalt started Game 2 of the NLDS against Cincinnati, two nights after Roy Halladay's no-hitter. The Reds chipped away and built a 4–0 lead in the fifth, but a comedy of errors allowed the Phillies to score five unearned runs and win the game. Oswalt then outpitched Jonathan Sanchez to win Game 2 of the NLCS against the Giants (allowing three hits and one run over eight innings), and allowed just one earned run in six frames in Game 6, but the Phillies' bats didn't support him in a 3–2 loss.

Oswalt has won more games since 2001 than any other National League pitcher, and his career ERA of 3.18 places him behind only Johan Santana among active starters with at least 1,000 innings pitched — ahead of Roy Halladay, Felix Hernandez and CC Sabathia. Those numbers give him the dubious honor of being the best pitcher never to win a Cy Young Award.

david
PRICE

TAMPA BAY RAYS ◆ AL East

David Price was so dominating in college that *Baseball America* said his "excellence almost defies words." He was a sure bet to go first in the 2007 draft, but no one could have guessed that 16 months later he would be pitching in the World Series.

Price grew up in Murfreesboro, Tennessee, and was a menacing six-foot-six in high school, where he first garnered the attention of scouts. The Dodgers selected him in the 19th round in 2004, but instead of signing he accepted a scholarship from Vanderbilt University in Nashville. His college career was legendary, and in his final year he was almost unhittable with a high-90s fastball and a nasty slider. Price went 11–1 that season with 194 strikeouts and only 31 walks in 133 innings. He carted home virtually all of college baseball's most prestigious trophies in 2007, including the Golden Spikes Award (best amateur player), the Roger Clemens Award (best college pitcher) and the Dick Howser Trophy (best college player). That year the Rays selected him first overall and handed him a $5.6 million signing bonus.

Price left college with more than a mantel full of hardware. A soft-spoken and shy kid when he arrived at Vanderbilt, Price also acquired the fierce competitive spirit he'd need to make it to the majors. As scouts like to say, there's never a shortage of lively arms at the college or minor league level; what's much more rare is what baseball people call "makeup," and Price had it.

In 2008, his first pro season, Price rose quickly from Class-A to Triple-A as he won his first 11 decisions. The Rays were impressed enough to make him a late-season call up while they were in the middle of a pennant race. Down the stretch, he pitched 14 innings, mostly in relief, allowed just nine hits and posted a stingy 1.93 ERA. The Rays shocked everyone by finishing first in the AL East.

When the Rays faced the Red Sox in the ALCS, manager Joe Maddon called on Price when Game 2

went to extra innings. The rookie closed out the 11th by getting two big outs, and then got his first big-league win when the Rays tallied in the bottom of the frame. The series eventually went to seven games, and in the deciding match the Rays took a 3–1 lead into the eighth, but the Sox loaded the bases with two out. With the left-handed J.D. Drew coming to the plate, Maddon called for Price again, and the 22-year-old showed remarkable composure as he struck out Drew to end the threat. Then he pitched a scoreless ninth to close out the win and earn his first save. With fewer than 20 innings of big-league experience, David Price found himself on the bottom of the dogpile as Tampa Bay celebrated their first trip to the World Series. Unfortunately for the Rays, the Phillies took the Fall Classic in five games, though Price pitched well, finishing two games and allowing just one earned run.

The Rays decided to groom Price as a starter in 2009, but he didn't make the team in spring training and opened the season in Triple-A. There he continued to improve his changeup to keep hitters off balance when they expected his heater. He returned to Tampa Bay that May, but didn't hit his stride until the second half, when he went 7–4. But thanks to an 11-game

losing skid in September, the Rays finished the season 84–78, well off their previous year's pace and out of the postseason.

Price was slated to be the number-four starter in 2010, but he quickly emerged as the ace. On April 25, he tossed his first shutout, blanking the Blue Jays on four hits while striking out nine. He won four straight starts in May, then four more in June, and by the break he was 12–4. Yankees' manager Joe Girardi selected him to start the All-Star Game, making Price the youngest to do so since Dwight Gooden in 1988.

The Rays stayed in contention all year, and during the September drive Price went 4–0 with a 1.67 ERA. Despite dropping five of their last eight games, Tampa finished first with 96 wins. But in the postseason against the Texas Rangers, Price went head-to-head with Cliff Lee twice and was outmatched both times. He had excellent command (no walks in 12 innings) but the Rangers tagged him for eight runs in the two games and the Rays dropped both by the same 5–1 score.

Price's regular-season numbers were the best ever by a Rays starter: a stellar 19–6 record with a 2.72 ERA, a 1.193 WHIP and 188 strikeouts in 208 innings. That November, he received four first-place votes and finished as the runner-up for the AL Cy Young Award.

Ticket

$ 24.95
GATE 17
SECTION **FIELD**
SEAT **E44**
B1AA472
24OCT11

CAREER HIGHLIGHTS

- pitched in the World Series 16 months after being drafted, faster than any other number-one pick
- only AL pitcher to rank in the top three in both wins and ERA in 2010
- named the starting pitcher of the 2010 AL All-Star Team

14 PITCHER

David PRICE

CC SABATHIA 52

Almost immediately after CC Sabathia began lighting up the American League with his blazing fastball in 2001, baseball pundits were predicting that either his arm or his temper would sideline his career before he could achieve stardom. And yet, a decade later, the lefty has become not only one of the most dominant pitchers in the game, but also a veritable workhorse: he has averaged almost 16 wins and more than 210 innings over the past 10 seasons.

Carsten Charles Sabathia grew up in Vallejo, California, in the Bay Area, where he was an outstanding high school athlete. At six-foot-seven he was tall enough to play basketball, but it was football and baseball where he excelled. By the time the Cleveland Indians drafted him in the first round in 1998, his fastball was already in the high 90s, and two years later he was the organization's best pitching prospect.

The 20-year-old Sabathia won the fourth spot in the Indians rotation in 2001, and although he was the youngest player in the American League, he was the Tribe's most dependable starter. The team was 24–9 when he took the mound, and he posted a magnificent 17–5 record with 171 strikeouts as the Indians won their sixth division title in seven years. That October, Sabathia became the youngest pitcher ever to start an ALDS match. He won the pivotal Game 3 to give the Indians the edge in the series, but they dropped the next two to the powerful Mariners.

Sabathia's immaturity was a problem early on. When the big lefty got into a jam, after one of his fielders booted a ball, or when he disagreed with an umpire's opinion of the strike zone, he could lose his composure. But he eventually learned to control both his emotions and his trademark fastball. He put it all together in 2007, when he was 19–7 with a 3.21 ERA, and led AL hurlers with 241 innings pitched. His control was astounding: he fanned a personal-best 209 and walked a career-low 37, far and away the best ratio in either league. The Indians went 96–66, tied for the best mark in the majors, and Sabathia took home the Cy Young Award. In the postseason, however, he was a major disappointment, racking up an 8.80 ERA in three starts, including a loss against the Red Sox in the pivotal Game 5 of the ALCS.

In July 2008, the Milwaukee Brewers acquired Sabathia in a trade as they tried to end a 26-year playoff drought. The southpaw was the best pitcher in baseball after the deal, posting a 1.65 ERA in 17 starts, including seven complete games and three shutouts. On August 31, he came within a whisker of a no-hitter against the Pirates — the only hit coming when Sabathia mishandled a check-swing dribbler that could have been ruled an error. He won the game that clinched the wild card for the Brewers, but flopped in his only postseason outing: the Phillies tagged him for five runs in Game 2 of the NLDS, including a grand slam by Shane Victorino.

His stay in Milwaukee was brief: Sabathia signed a long-term deal with the Yankees before the 2009 season. With a monster second half that year (11–2 with a 2.74 ERA in 15 starts) he won 19 games and paced the Yankees to a first-place finish and his third straight postseason appearance, each with different teams. Sabathia quickly vanquished his reputation for choking in the playoffs. He won Game 1 of the ALDS against the Minnesota Twins, then beat the Angels twice in the Championship Series. He gave up a single earned run in each start, walked three and struck out 20 in just under 23 innings.

In Game 1 of the World Series against Philadelphia, Sabathia allowed just four hits and two runs over seven innings, but his friend and former teammate Cliff Lee silenced the Yankees in a 6–1 Phillies win. He pitched well again in Game 4, which the Bronx Bombers won before completing their 29th World Series championship three days later. Sabathia was 3–1 with a 1.98 ERA in the postseason, holding his opponents to no more than three runs in all five outings and never leaving before the seventh inning.

Sabathia finally became a 20-game winner in 2010. From June onwards, he was a fearsome 18–5 with a 2.76 ERA, and he finished the year with a major-league-leading 21 victories. Back in the playoffs for the fourth straight time, Sabathia won both of his decisions, albeit with lots of help from Yankee lumber. He surrendered 10 runs in only 16 innings for a 5.63 ERA. After the season, Sabathia needed arthroscopic surgery to repair his right knee, and some wondered whether the injury had played a role in his postseason struggles. But the big man brushed aside the concerns: CC Sabathia is not one to make excuses, and with career numbers like his, he doesn't have to.

$ 24.95
GATE 31
SECTION FIELD
SEAT P44
D6AB437
12OCT11

CAREER HIGHLIGHTS

- leads the majors in wins (157) since making his debut in 2001
- ranked first in the majors with 1,026 strikeouts from 2006 through 2010
- AL Cy Young Award winner in 2007

52 PITCHER

CC SABATHIA

johan
SANTANA

NEW YORK METS ◆ NL East

When Johan Santana was 15, he thought he might like to become an electrician like his dad. Johan played for his local team in the remote town of Tovar, Venezuela, but he didn't think of baseball as a potential career. Then one day an intrepid scout for the Houston Astros rented a car and drove for 10 hours through the Andes to the Santana family home. The scout handed the wide-eyed teenager a baseball autographed by the 1994 Astros and invited Johan to the team's training facility. A decade later, major-league batters were wishing that scout's car had broken down on the way.

Santana signed with the Astros following the 1995 draft and spent four years in their farm system, but he was eventually acquired by the Minnesota Twins. He debuted in 2000 at the age of 21 and made five starts and 25 relief appearances that season, posting an unimpressive 6.49 ERA. The Twins returned Santana to the minors, where a pitching coach helped him develop his signature changeup.

Once back in the big leagues, Santana made his case for a spot in the rotation by going 11–2 with a 2.85 ERA over 18 starts in 2003, helping the Twins to a division title. Manager Rod Gardenhire even handed him the ball for Game 1 of the ALDS against the Yankees. He was brilliant in the first four innings, but had to leave because of a cramped hamstring. When he valiantly tried to come back for Game 4, the Yankees pummeled him, winning the match and the series.

Santana had offseason surgery to remove bone chips from his elbow, and it hampered his performance early in 2004. But once he was healthy, he showed complete control of a late-breaking slider as well as his fastball and devastating changeup. Santana suddenly began to flourish. In the second half, he was an astounding 13–0 and carried the team to its third straight AL Central title. He won 20 games and led the AL in WHIP (0.92) and strikeouts, fanning 265 while issuing only 54 walks. Santana pitched seven scoreless innings to lead the Twins to a 2–0 win in Game 1 of the ALDS, but the Yankees swept the next three to take the series. In November, Santana received all 28 first-place votes and took home his first Cy Young Award.

In 2005 and 2006, Santana continued to be the most feared hurler in the league. With supreme command of all his pitches, he allowed less than one base runner per inning in both seasons, won back-to-back strikeout crowns and posted a combined 2.82 ERA. He was 35–13 over the two seasons, including an astonishing 19–3 after the All-Star break. By the end of 2006, his lifetime winning percentage was .716, the second-best in MLB history at the time. He was again a unanimous choice for the Cy Young Award in 2006.

The Twins traded their ace lefty to the Mets in 2008, and Santana went on to have three challenging seasons. In his first campaign in New York, he split his first 14 decisions but didn't lose a game from July onwards, going 9–0 with a 2.09 ERA in the final three months. He led the majors in ERA (2.53) and innings pitched (234), and he passed 200 strikeouts for the fifth season in a row. His crowning moment came on September 27, when he tossed a three-hit shutout against the Marlins on three days' rest, as the Mets battled for a postseason berth. It turned out that he had done so despite a torn meniscus in his left knee, which required surgery before the end of the season.

Santana's first seven games of 2009 added up to the best start to a season by any Mets pitcher in franchise history. He allowed just four earned runs and struck out 60 batters over 46 frames, but still managed to lose two of those games because of unearned runs. Santana allowed three hits or fewer six times that season and lost three of those starts, and he deserved better than his 13–9 record. In mid-August doctors found multiple bone fragments in his left elbow, and he needed season-ending arthroscopic surgery to remove them.

Santana won 11 games in 2010, his fewest since becoming a full-time starter, though again he deserved more. He held opposing hitters to a .199 average and he did not allow a run in 8 of his 29 starts. In August he pitched three consecutive complete games — the first Met to do that in 20 years — but lost two of them. For the third straight year, Santana had to cut his season short. On September 5, he took himself out of the game after experiencing soreness and went under the knife again, this time for a torn shoulder ligament that will likely force him to miss at least part of the 2011 season.

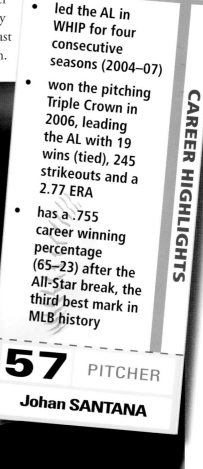

$ 24.95
GATE 15
SECTION CLUB
SEAT A24
A4ZE354
6AUG11

- led the AL in WHIP for four consecutive seasons (2004–07)

- won the pitching Triple Crown in 2006, leading the AL with 19 wins (tied), 245 strikeouts and a 2.77 ERA

- has a .755 career winning percentage (65–23) after the All-Star break, the third best mark in MLB history

CAREER HIGHLIGHTS

57   PITCHER

Johan SANTANA

justin VERLANDER 35

DETROIT TIGERS ◆ AL Central

Only a handful of big-league hurlers can hit the magic number 100 on a radar gun, and fewer still can do it six or seven innings into a game. Not only is Justin Verlander one of these rare fireballers, he also has a second lethal weapon. When *Baseball America* polled MLB managers in 2010, they rated Verlander's fastball and curveball the best in the American League. When he's in command of both, hitters don't have a chance.

Justin Verlander was Detroit's first-round pick in the 2004 draft and he raced through their minor-league system. In 2005 he was a combined 11–2 with a 1.29 ERA in Class-A and Double-A and was called up to the majors before the season was out. In spring training of 2006, Verlander threw well enough to win the fifth spot in the starting rotation. In his first outing that season, he gave up two hits over seven scoreless innings, won four straight starts in May, and by August he was 14–4. Verlander's success came as much from his savvy as from

his stuff: he thought through each at-bat like a veteran and knew more than one way to get a batter out.

The Tigers clinched the wild card berth in 2006, and Verlander started Game 2 of the ALDS against the Yankees, getting a no-decision after allowing three runs and leaving in the sixth. He beat Oakland in Game 2 of the Championship Series, though his four runs in less than six frames was hardly vintage Verlander. When the Tigers advanced to the World Series, the Cardinals battered him for six runs in five innings in the opening game. He got the start again in the decisive Game 5 and pitched his best game of the

$ 24.95
GATE 36
SECTION FIELD
SEAT N12
B4SP548
8 JULY 11

CAREER HIGHLIGHTS

- named AL Rookie of the Year in 2006 (17–9, 3.63 ERA)
- one of two pitchers to have won Rookie of the Year, played in a World Series and pitched a no-hitter before age 25
- three-time AL All-Star (2007, 2009, 2010)

35 PITCHER
Justin VERLANDER

postseason, but a pair of unearned runs sunk the Tigers and the rookie was tagged with the loss again. In four postseason games, his ERA was 5.82, and many put his spotty performance down to fatigue.

But if Verlander's arm was overworked in 2006, he showed no sign of it the following season. He did not surrender an earned run in his first two outings, and had won six of eight decisions by June 12, when the Tigers hosted Milwaukee for an interleague game at Comerica Park. Verlander and Brewers starter Jeff Suppan locked horns in a classic pitchers' duel that stood at 1–0 until the sixth inning. Verlander had not allowed a hit to that point, and one of his fastballs was clocked at 102 miles per hour. Fans inched toward the edge of their seats after Magglio Ordonez made a sliding grab of a line drive in the seventh, and then the infield turned a nifty double play to erase a one-out walk in the eighth. Verlander needed seven pitches in the ninth to blow away Craig Counsell and Tony Graffanino, leaving only J.J. Hardy to deal with. Verlander quickly got in front 0–2 before Hardy hit a curveball high into right field. It landed harmlessly in Ordonez's glove, and the 24-year-old had his no-hitter — the first by a Detroit pitcher in 23 years.

Verlander proved he could handle a 200-inning workload in 2007, and he finished the season with a stellar 18–6 record, a 3.66 ERA and 183 strikeouts. But after two brilliant seasons to start his career, the righty had a year he'd prefer to forget. He enjoyed a span of eight starts in which he went 6–0 with a 2.30 ERA, but that was sandwiched between two dismal stretches. He opened the season 1–7, and then from late July to late September he lost eight times in 11 starts and stacked up an ERA close to 7.00. He led the majors with 17 losses in 2008.

Tigers fans must have worried that Verlander had permanently lost his touch after he was bombed in three of his first four starts in 2009. But after that inauspicious beginning, the righty rebounded with an outstanding season. From late April to mid-June, he won seven straight decisions, compiling a 1.10 ERA and 81 strikeouts over nine outings. In his 35 starts, he allowed one run or less 12 times, and he fanned at least eight batters 20 times. Verlander was all over the leader board in 2009, leading the majors with 240 innings pitched, 269 K's, and a strikeout rate of 10.1 per nine innings. He also tied Felix Hernandez and CC Sabathia for the AL lead with 19 wins against nine losses.

Verlander's 2010 numbers were very similar. He improved his ERA a few points to a career-best 3.37, tossed four complete games, struck out 219 batters, and passed the 200-inning threshold for the fourth straight year. A five-game winning streak beginning in late August helped him compile an 18–9 record. Two seasons after Verlander lost 17 games, he surpassed that figure in the win column for the fourth time in his young career.

adam WAINWRIGHT 50

ST. LOUIS CARDINALS ◆ NL Central

A dam Wainwright was nine years old the year Bobby Cox began his second tenure as manager of the Atlanta Braves. The Wainwrights lived in Brunswick, Georgia, and cheered on their team as Cox led them to five National League pennants in nine seasons. Adam imagined that someday he'd be standing on the mound in a Braves uniform and pitching in a World Series, and he got one step closer to that dream when his beloved Braves drafted him in the second round in 2000.

The six-foot-seven right-hander spent the 2003 season with the Double-A Greenville Braves, where he won 10 games and posted a 3.37 ERA. That earned him a promotion for 2004, but it would not be in the Atlanta organization. In the offseason, the Braves traded Wainwright to the St. Louis Cardinals. He was heartbroken, but the timing turned out to be fortunate: the Cards were a team on the rise and, as it turned out, Wainwright would play a huge role in their success.

Wainwright was impressive enough in spring training in 2006 to win a major-league job. Manager Tony La Russa used him as a setup man for the Cards' veteran closer, Jason Isringhausen, and Wainwright thrived in this underappreciated role, earning 23 holds and suffering only one loss in 61 appearances. Then, in early September, he got an unexpected opportunity when Isringhausen suffered a season-ending hip injury and La Russa asked Wainwright to step in for the final three weeks of the season. He embraced the stopper's role and helped the Cardinals edge

$ 24.95
GATE **44**
SECTION **FIELD**
SEAT **T58**
A9TS284
13AUG11

CAREER HIGHLIGHTS

- homered in his first major-league at bat and then pitched three innings for the win (May 24, 2006)

- his 2.68 ERA is second only to Roy Halladay (2.67) since 2008

- amassed more than 210 strikeouts in both 2009 and 2010

50 PITCHER

Adam WAINWRIGHT

the Astros for the NL Central crown.

In his first postseason the rookie showed remarkable composure. He tossed the final inning of all three Cardinals wins in the ALDS against the Padres and earned another save in Game 5 of the Championship Series with the Mets. New York then won the next match to force a Game 7. The Cards were up 3–1 heading to the bottom of the ninth and Wainwright jogged to the mound to close it out. He certainly made things interesting. He allowed a pair of leadoff singles, and then a two-out walk to load the bases for Mets' slugger Carlos Beltran, owner of 41 home runs that season. Wainwright got in front 0–2 and then snapped off a wicked curveball that froze Beltran for strike three and sent the Cardinals to the World Series.

Facing the Detroit Tigers in Game 4 of the Fall Classic, Wainwright allowed the tying run to score on a Brandon Inge double in the eighth. But the Cards took the lead in the ninth, and Wainwright wound up with the win. The next night, with the Redbirds looking to clinch the series, Wainwright entered the ninth inning with a 4–2 lead. After a hit and a two-out walk, Inge strode to the plate with another opportunity to tie the game. But this time the rookie closer blew him away on three pitches. Wainwright threw his arms in the air as he was mobbed by his teammates, and his expression betrayed not only joy, but disbelief. In all, he had pitched 9 ⅔ scoreless innings in October and was on the mound for the final out of all three playoff series.

Despite his remarkable success in the closer's role, La Russa made Wainwright his number-two starter in 2007, behind Chris Carpenter. As it happened, Carpenter was lost to injury after Opening Day, and Wainwright ended up leading the staff with 14 wins, 32 starts and 202 innings pitched. He missed almost half of 2008 with a sprained finger on his right hand, but still managed to go 11–3 with a 3.20 ERA.

By 2009, Wainwright had built himself into one of the game's elite starters. That year he won 19 games, tops in the majors, including a 12–1 mark on the road. His final road victory was the division-clinching match against the Colorado Rockies at Coors Field. That November, he won a Gold Glove and received more first-place votes (12 out of 30) for the Cy Young Award than both Carpenter (9) and Tim Lincecum (11), but the Giants hurler took home the prize on overall points.

Wainwright made another run at the Cy Young in 2010 after nailing down his first 20-win season and posting a career-best 2.42 ERA. However, just as spring training opened in 2011, the Cards announced that Wainwright would miss the season due to Tommy John surgery.

jered WEAVER

LOS ANGELES ANGELS OF ANAHEIM ◆ AL West

Jered Weaver's brother Jeff is six years his senior, so the two were too far apart in age to be rivals growing up. Jered was still in high school when Jeff broke into the majors, and the elder Weaver's career was already well established when Jered set the college baseball world on fire in 2004. But two years later, the two were teammates with the Los Angeles Angels of Anaheim — until Jered took his big brother's job.

The Weavers were raised in Simi Valley, California, just outside the City of Angels. Jered attended Long Beach State, where he had a magical college career. During his senior year in 2004, he racked up a 15–1 record and a 1.62 ERA while fanning 213 batters and walking just 21 in 144 innings. Weaver would almost surely have been the first overall pick in the draft that year, but he and super-agent Scott Boras made it clear they were looking for an astronomical signing bonus. That scared off many teams, and the Angels were able to select Weaver with the 12th pick. The negotiations dragged on for 11 months — Weaver was the longest draft holdout in MLB history — before the pitcher agreed to $4 million.

Weaver's big-league debut in 2006 was a gem. He twirled seven shutout innings against the Baltimore Orioles, allowing three hits and one walk in a 10–1 rout. He joined his brother Jeff in the Angels' starting rotation for a month that year, during which he won all four starts, but then was shipped back to the minors to make room for Bartolo Colon, who returned from the DL in June.

Within a couple of weeks the Angels realized that Jered was ready for a full-time job, and that made his elder brother expendable. The club dealt Jeff to the St. Louis Cardinals and recalled their star rookie. Jered was simply brilliant for the rest of the season, winning his first three starts after being recalled, and after three no-decisions he won twice more. By August 18 he was 9–0, tying Whitey Ford's 56-year-old American League record for most consecutive victories at the beginning of a career.

Weaver ended his rookie season at 11–2 with a 2.56 ERA and 105 strikeouts in 19 games. (That October, Jered was on hand at Busch Stadium to watch Jeff win the deciding game of the World Series.)

In his second season in 2007, Weaver was 13–7 and got his first postseason experience when the Angels won 94 games and placed first in the AL West. He started Game 3 of the ALDS against Boston and held his own until David Ortiz and Manny Ramirez tagged him for back-to-back jacks in the fourth. Weaver left the game in the sixth with the score still close at 2–0, but the bullpen fell apart: the Angels lost 9–1 and were swept in the series.

On June 28, 2008, in an interleague game against the Dodgers, Weaver was involved in one of the oddest games of the season. He did not allow a hit over six innings, but in the fifth the Dodgers scored on two errors, a stolen base and a sacrifice fly. Angels' reliever Jose Arredondo then pitched the next two innings without surrendering a hit, but his teammates could not score, and Weaver ended up tagged with a loss in an unofficial no-hitter.

The Angels' 2009 season opened with a tragedy when the team's 22-year-old rookie Nick Adenhart was killed in a car crash just hours after making his first start of the year. Weaver was scheduled to pitch the next day, and he wrote his friend's initials in the dirt on the mound, a ritual he repeated all season. Pitching with a heavy heart, he battled into the seventh inning and allowed only one unearned run as he beat the Red Sox 6–3.

That June, Weaver had another emotional start when he faced his brother Jeff, now pitching with the Los Angeles Dodgers. Jered surrendered 10 hits and six runs before being driven from the game in the sixth, and Jeff got the victory in a 6–4 Dodgers win. Weaver went 16–8 with a 3.75 ERA in 2009, with four complete games, including a pair of shutouts, and he pitched an outstanding Game 2 in the ALDS to help the Angels sweep the Red Sox. In the offseason, he received the inaugural Nick Adenhart Award as the team's pitcher of the year.

With the departure of John Lackey before the 2010 season, Weaver became the ace of the Angels staff and was consistently effective all year. In a league-leading 34 starts, he logged 224 innings, posted a 3.01 ERA and a 1.074 WHIP, and led the majors with 233 punchouts. But his offense offered paltry support: in half of his starts, the Angels produced three runs or fewer, and he wound up 13–12, a record that didn't reflect the performance of a veteran pitcher who has never played little brother to anyone.

HEATH BELL - San Diego Padres

FRANCISCO CORDERO - Cincinnati Reds

JONATHAN PAPELBON - Boston Red Sox

MARIANO RIVERA - New York Yankees

BRIAN WILSON - San Francisco Giants

FIREMEN

heath
BELL

SAN DIEGO PADRES ◆ NL West

For as long as anyone could remember, the tolling of AC/DC's "Hells Bells" signaled Trevor Hoffman's entry from the San Diego bullpen. Baseball's all-time leader in saves closed out 761 games for the Padres during his tenure, and when he departed in 2009, his job fell to a 31-year-old who had never occupied the high-pressure role on a major-league team. But it didn't take long for Padres fans to take to their new closer. For San Diego's opponents, the ninth inning has become Bell's hell.

Heath Bell was born in Oceanside, California, and attended Santiago Canyon College, where he was a freshman All-American in 1997. Tampa Bay drafted him in the 69th round that year, but he didn't sign. When he went undrafted the following year, the New York Mets inked a deal with him as an amateur free agent.

Many pitchers come to the role later in their career, but Bell has always been a reliever, and even in college he relished the closer's role. His money pitch was his fastball, but he also threw a good changeup and sharp curveball. As he worked his way through the Mets' farm system, he recorded 48 saves at the Class-A level, but his road through the minors proved long and grueling: he worked in 254 games over six seasons before finally cracking the Mets' lineup late in 2004 at the age of 26.

Over the next three seasons, Bell bounced between the majors and Triple-A, as the Mets could not seem to find a role for him. Braden Looper and Billy Wagner owned the

$ 24.95
GATE 19
SECTION CLUB
SEAT E45
S4RD173
18AUG11

CAREER HIGHLIGHTS

• led the majors with a combined 89 saves in 2009 and 2010

• received back-to-back Rolaids Relief Man Awards (2009 and 2010)

• two-time NL All-Star (2009 and 2010)

21 RELIEF PITCHER

Heath BELL

closer's job during those years, and Bell toiled in middle relief. He was grateful when the Mets dealt him to the Padres after the 2006 season — at least in San Diego he might have an opportunity to be useful.

The move turned out to be a renaissance for Bell. The Padres used him primarily as a setup man for Hoffman, and he thrived in the new role. In 2007 he appeared in 81 games, posted a 2.02 ERA, and held batters to a .185 average. By stranding more than 80 percent of runners he inherited, he amassed 32 holds and set the table for Hoffman's 42 saves. That year, Bell led all MLB relievers with 93 $^{2}/_{3}$ innings pitched and 102 strikeouts. The following season his numbers dipped a bit, but he still led the club with 24 holds in 74 appearances in 2008.

The club could not come to terms with Hoffman after the 2008 campaign, and their legendary closer left to join the Milwaukee Brewers. That presented a glorious opportunity for Bell, and the big righty set about preparing himself. He claims he lost 25 pounds using his daughter's Wii Fit video game, and dropping that extra weight may have given a boost to his fastball.

In his first 16 appearances in the closer's role in 2009, Bell was virtually untouchable. He did not allow a run over 17 innings, struck out 22 and limited opponents to a .125 average. He was a perfect 11-for-11 in save opportunities by mid-May. The fourth and fifth were the sweetest, as they came against the club that gave up on him: they were the first two saves recorded at the Mets' new Citi Field.

The Padres played .500 ball for the first two months in 2009, but they plummeted out of contention with a 17–37 record in June and July and finished the year with just 75 wins. Their one consolation was that, if they could take a lead into the ninth, it was usually secure. Bell led the National League with 42 saves in 48 opportunities and compiled a 2.71 ERA in 68 games.

With a much improved team in 2010, the Padres hoped for much better results, and they got them. San Diego was near the top of the NL West from mid-April onwards and contended all season long. Over the first two months, Bell's ERA was 1.17 and he converted 14 of 17 save opportunities. After that he didn't blow a save for the rest of the season as he helped the Padres build a 6½ game lead by August 25. But then the club went on a miserable 10-game losing skid and the lead evaporated. That set up a dramatic series against the Giants on the final weekend of the regular season: the Padres were two games back and needed a sweep. They won the first two, with Bell getting saves in both, but fell one game short.

While Bell would have loved a postseason berth, his individual numbers were outstanding: he logged 47 saves (second only to Brian Wilson's 48) and led all MLB closers by converting 94 percent of his opportunities. He was 6–1 with a 1.93 ERA and was scored on in only 15 of his 67 appearances, including a solitary home run. Heath Bell had enormous shoes to fill in San Diego, but after waiting 11 professional seasons for the opportunity to become an everyday closer, he's found a home.

francisco CORDERO

The Cincinnati Reds were desperate for help after their 2007 season, when they racked up 90 losses. It wasn't so much the number of defeats, but the circumstances of those defeats. The Reds bullpen had an appalling 5.17 ERA, the worst in the National League, and blew 27 save opportunities. Losing so many heartbreakers was demoralizing, so before the 2008 campaign kicked off, the Reds went out and acquired Francisco Cordero to stop the bleeding.

Cordero was born in Santo Domingo, Dominican Republic, and selected by Detroit in the 1994 draft. He spent only a brief stint with the Tigers: he was called up in August 1999 and didn't allow a run in his first 11 big-league appearances, most of which were as a seventh-inning set-up man. But at the end of that season, the Tigers sent Cordero to the Texas Rangers in a deal to acquire superstar slugger Juan Gonzalez.

During his first year in Arlington, he made 56 relief appearances with mixed results, and then missed almost all of the 2001 season with a stress fracture in his back. He yo-yoed between Triple-A and the Rangers in 2002, but managed to pick up 10 saves in 39 appearances and finish the year with a sparkling 1.79 ERA.

Cordero's career blossomed in 2004, his first year as a full-time closer. He was perfect in converting his first 19 save opportunities before finally blowing a lead on June 15. He later had another string of 21 consecutive saves to set a franchise record, bringing his season total to 49, second only to Mariano Rivera in the American League. He collected 37 more the following season, but 2006 proved more difficult. He had a rough April — he blew five ninth-inning leads in a span of eight games — and by July the Rangers had run Cordero out of town by trading him to the Milwaukee Brewers.

When Cordero relocated to Milwaukee, his mother encouraged him to start wearing a bracelet she had given to him during his difficult months in Texas. Whether or not the religious symbols made the difference — Cordero

insists they did — the closer turned his season around in his new home. He allowed only five runs in 28 appearances with Milwaukee in 2006, picking up 16 saves in just over two months. When the Brewers turned themselves into contenders the following year, Cordero was a big reason. He had saved his first 22 opportunities of the year (with a 0.36 ERA) before the Brewers played an interleague series against his former club at Rangers Ballpark. In the opener, Cordero came on in the ninth to protect a 3–0 lead and quickly got two outs to silence the Texas crowd. But then he surrendered five hits and a walk and allowed the Rangers to roar back and win 4–3. The next day, he blew another save in the bottom of the ninth. Texas fans had fun razzing him, but Cordero had the last laugh. He logged a club-record 44 saves in 2007 and earned his second All-Star selection.

That's when the Reds called on the portly right-hander to be their savior. The club handed Cordero a four-year deal worth $46 million, and he shouldered a huge load in his first season: he finished a club-record 63 games in 2008 and logged all 34 of the team's saves. But while he started and finished strong, Cordero's performance from mid-May to mid-

August was mediocre (4.85 ERA and six blown saves). The Reds under new manager Dusty Baker showed little overall improvement and won just two games more than the previous season.

Cordero returned to his All-Star form in 2009 with 39 saves in 43 attempts (91 percent) while lowering his ERA to 2.16, his best mark in five seasons. He didn't surrender a lead until mid-June, which finally broke off a string of 29 consecutive saves going back to the end of 2008. His last save of the season on September 24 was the 250th of his career.

Cincinnati's fortunes changed dramatically in 2010, when they won 91 games and finished atop the NL Central for the first time in 15 years. Cordero posted an impressive 40 saves, though he had his struggles, reflected in his 3.84 ERA and 1.431 WHIP. He squandered leads in some important September games, and even when he did nail down victory he often made things exciting. As the Reds headed to the postseason, some even wondered whether the closer's role should go to Aroldis Chapman, the Reds' rookie with the otherworldly fastball. In the end, it didn't matter — the Phillies steamrolled over the Reds in the NLDS and Cincinnati never had a ninth-inning lead to protect.

$ 24.95
GATE 42
SECTION FIELD
SEAT H33
D2DE672
8SEPT11

CAREER HIGHLIGHTS

- ranks third among all active relievers with 290 career saves
- one of only 11 pitchers to record 100 saves in both leagues
- three-time All-Star (2004, 2007, 2009)

48 RELIEF PITCHER

Francisco CORDERO

jonathan
PAPELBON

BOSTON RED SOX ◆ AL East

For Red Sox fans, the defining image of the 2007 postseason will always be the dance. While celebrating on the Fenway infield after Boston clinched the AL East, the cameras caught Jonathan Papelbon dancing an Irish jig while clad only in a T-shirt and Spandex shorts. When the Sox won the pennant a few weeks later, he performed his postgame footwork again. And when the team won it all, Papelbon donned a kilt for the World Series parade and did his victory dance on a flatbed truck as it rolled through Beantown.

The hard-throwing righty had starred as both a starter and a closer at Mississippi State University, but when he made his major-league debut in July 2005, it was in the former capacity. He was shifted to the bullpen later in the season, and when spring training began in 2006, it wasn't clear what Papelbon's job would be. The Red Sox already had a closer in Keith

Foulke, one of the playoff heroes of 2004, and their starting rotation was strong as well. But Papelbon was so impressive out of the bullpen in April that he usurped the closer's role. Using a toxic mixture of fastballs in the high 90s, sliders and splitters, he compiled 35 saves by September 1, when the Sox shut him down because of soreness in his shoulder. His season ended with a 0.92 ERA, a 0.78 WHIP and 75 strikeouts in 68 innings.

The shoulder was completely healthy to start 2007, and Papelbon was remarkably effective all season. With Hideki Okajima as the setup man (the rookie left-hander racked up 26 holds) and Papelbon throwing the ninth, the Red Sox rarely lost in the late innings as they cruised to a 96–66 record and the AL East title.

In the postseason that year, Papelbon saved Game 2 of the Division Series against the Angels, and clinched Game 7 of the ALCS against the Indians with a two-

CAREER HIGHLIGHTS

- owns a career 2.22 ERA, the lowest among all active pitchers (minimum 350 innings)

- only pitcher in MLB history to record 35 or more saves in his first five full seasons (2006–10)

- four-time AL All-Star (2006–09)

RELIEF PITCHER

58

Jonathan PAPELBON

inning save to preserve a 5–2 Red Sox win. But he saved his best stuff for the Fall Classic. In Game 2, with the Red Sox up 2–1 in the eighth, the Colorado Rockies' Matt Holliday singled to put the tying run on base, but Papelbon promptly picked him off to end the inning. He then worked a one-two-three ninth to earn the save. He closed out the third match as well, and then found himself with a chance to clinch a championship the following night, when he trotted out to protect a 4–3 lead in Game 4. After finishing the eighth and retiring the first two batters in the ninth, all that stood between Papelbon and his first World Series ring was pinch hitter Seth Smith. The Rockies outfielder swung through a 2–2 fastball, and Papelbon leaped off the mound to embrace catcher Jason Varitek.

The young closer's performance just got better over the next two seasons. Papelbon logged a career-high 41 saves in 2008, and 38 more the following year. Over his first four seasons as a full-time closer, his pitching line ranked among

the best of all time: 151 saves, a 1.74 ERA, a WHIP of 0.917, 312 strikeouts and just 60 walks in 264 innings. Since 1900, only one pitcher with more than 200 innings had a better career ERA than Papelbon did in his first five campaigns.

Papelbon continued twirling his postseason magic in 2008, when he appeared in seven of Boston's 11 playoff games, picking up a win and three saves in 10 $^1/_3$ scoreless innings. When he tossed a perfect frame in Game 2 of the 2009 Division Series against the Los Angeles Angels, Papelbon ran his streak to 26 consecutive playoff innings without allowing a run. He finally proved mortal in Game 3, by which time the Red Sox were already trailing the series two games to none. They hoped to force a Game 4 when they called on Papelbon to preserve a 6–4 advantage in the ninth, and he promptly retired the first two Angels hitters. But then Erick Aybar singled and Chone Figgins walked to bring the go-ahead run to the plate. Bobby Abreu then doubled to bring home a run, and Vlad Guerrero plated two more with a clutch single that would stand up as the series winner.

Although he amassed 37 saves in 2010, Papelbon wasn't quite the lights-out closer he had been to that point. He set career-highs with seven losses and eight blown saves, and had a particularly hard time in June, and again in September when his ERA was north of 10.00 over his final nine appearances.

With young fireballer Daniel Bard already on the roster, Boston added even more depth to their bullpen by acquiring Bobby Jenks from the White Sox and Dan Wheeler from the Rays before the start of the 2011 season. For the first time in his big-league career, Jonathan Papelbon may have to prove he can still dance.

mariano RIVERA

NEW YORK YANKEES ◆ AL East

$ 24.95
GATE 54
SECTION UPPER
SEAT G1
E3VE400
21MAY11

CAREER HIGHLIGHTS

- owns the second-lowest ERA (2.23) of any pitcher in MLB history (minimum 1,000 innings)

- all-time AL leader in saves (559), with 42 more in the postseason

- earned 11 All-Star selections and has saved four All-Star Games

42 RELIEF PITCHER
Mariano **RIVERA**

Mariano Rivera once told a sportswriter that his cut fastball was a gift from God. For more than 15 seasons, however, opposing batters have considered it a curse from the devil. The legendary closer known as Mo can throw a standard four-seam fastball and the odd changeup, but he is perhaps baseball's most successful one-trick pony. Hitters know the cutter is coming, but they're still helpless as it breaks several inches to the left as it crosses the plate, leaving a forest of broken bats in its wake.

Rivera's career with the Yankees began unremarkably as a starter in 1995. The following season, he worked as a setup man for John Wetteland and was so successful (130 strikeouts, 2.09 ERA) that he placed third in the Cy Young voting. When Wetteland became a free agent in the offseason, the Yankees moved Rivera into the closer's role. He struggled there at first — he blew three of his first six opportunities — but went on to record 43 saves and a 1.88 ERA in 1997.

In the ALDS that October, however, he coughed up a game-tying homer to Cleveland's Sandy Alomar in the eighth inning of Game 4. That blow turned the tide, and the Indians won the game and the next two to take the series. Rivera would have plenty of playoff opportunities to atone for that misstep.

In 1998 and 1999, Rivera made it three straight seasons with an ERA under 2.00, amassing 36 and 45 saves respectively. The Yankees steamrolled through the postseason and captured the World Series in both years. Rivera was magnificent in those playoffs. He did not allow an earned run in 25 $^2/_3$ innings and saved 12 of New York's 22 victories, earning World Series MVP honors in 1999. When the Yankees made it three in a row in 2000, Rivera added six more saves. Indeed, it's Mo's October dominance that has made him the best closer in the history of the game. Although Trevor Hoffman has recorded more regular-season saves, no one can touch Rivera's postseason success: in 94 appearances he has logged 42 saves (both MLB records that won't be broken in the foreseeable future) and is 8–1 with a 0.71 ERA.

Ironically, Rivera's two greatest regular-season save totals — 50 in 2001, and 53 in 2004 — were followed by his lowest October moments. His only postseason defeat came in Game 7 of the 2001 World Series against Arizona, when Luis Gonzalez's soft liner went over the drawn-in infield and plated the winning run in the bottom of the ninth. Rivera also blew three save opportunities in the 2004 postseason, most famously in Games 4 and 5 of the ALCS against the Red Sox. (In the fifth match, he merely allowed an inherited runner to score on a sacrifice fly.) Boston went on to win both games in extra innings, setting the stage for their eventual World Series triumph.

When the Yankees and Red Sox met again to open the 2005 regular season, Rivera blew saves in his first two appearances. But anyone who thought he had lost his nerve was soon proven wrong. Rivera did not fail in another save opportunity until mid-August (at one point nailing down 31 in a row), and finished the year with 43 saves and a stunning 1.38 ERA, the best mark of his career.

Rivera's 2007 campaign was decidedly mediocre by his standards: a 3.15 ERA and 30 saves for a team that won 94 games. Given that he was 37 years old, it was easy to think that Mo's best years were behind him. But somehow Rivera strung together three more miraculous seasons. In 2008, he saved 39 games in 40 chances with a 1.40 ERA and a freakishly low WHIP of 0.665. His control was impeccable. In 73 innings he struck out 77 batters and walked just six, for a ratio of almost 13-to-1. No pitcher had had strikeout-to-walk numbers like that since Hall of Famer Dennis Eckersley in his prime.

During the 2009 season, Rivera once again was a key figure in a Yankees World Series championship. Over his final 40 appearances, beginning in mid-June, he converted 30 of 31 save opportunities and posted a 0.68 ERA. In the postseason, Mo made 12 appearances, went 5-for-5 in saves (two of them needing six outs), and surrendered just one run in 16 innings. For the fourth time in his career, Rivera got the final out of the clinching games in all three postseason series.

Rivera continued to break bats and hearts in 2010, logging another 33 saves in his tenth season with an ERA under 2.00, and adding three more postseason saves to extend his all-time record. Two weeks after his 41st birthday, the ageless wonder inked a two-year deal that will likely allow him to end his career in the Bronx — before he's immortalized in Cooperstown.

brian WILSON

Closers have the highest-pressure job in baseball. If they save 9 out of 10 games, fans will always remember the one that got away. That's why relievers often look downright mean on the mound during those ninth-inning battles. As Brian Wilson once told a reporter: "When I'm on the field, my one thought is to completely annihilate you and do everything in my power to make you fail."

Wilson is undeniably eccentric. At the 2010 All-Star Game, the fireballing right-hander went to the mound wearing cleats so orange they looked like traffic cones. (He was later fined for the fashion faux-pas.) Later that season, Wilson grew a thick beard that seemed to be an homage to legendary closers Bruce Sutter and Jeff Reardon. What made the beard unique, however, was that Wilson dyed it jet-black — with shoe polish, it seemed. That made it stand out against his brown hair, a mixture of mullet and Mohawk. As the surprising Giants headed to the postseason in

2010, Wilson's facial hair became an icon and the inspiration for a slogan: "Fear the Beard."

But while his antics make headlines, Brian Wilson is no nutcase. He's a highly intelligent, affable, and well-liked man who excels at chess, crossword puzzles and trivia. Of course, his teammates know not to compete against him, because he always wins. Wilson developed his competitive spirit as a teenager, when he lost his father to cancer. Watching his dad endure that illness, Brian developed a maturity and fearlessness — not to mention some bottled-up anger — that would serve him well in his career.

Wilson was drafted by the Giants in 2003, though he didn't pitch that year as he recovered from Tommy John surgery. He suffered another injury in his first major-league game in April 2006, and during four stints in the majors that season, he posted a 5.40 ERA. He spent most of the 2007 season in Triple-A, but when the Giants recalled him in August, he was phenomenal: in his first 22 appearances, he held opponents to a .151 average and boasted an ERA of 0.84.

That performance earned Wilson a full-time job in 2008. Despite a 4.62 ERA that season, he picked up 41 saves for the Giants — second in the National League — and earned his first trip to the All-Star Game. From early May through mid-August, Wilson converted 24 consecutive save opportunities, the second-longest streak in team history.

Wilson got his ERA down to a much more respectable 2.74 in 2009, as he continued to be one of the elite closers in the league. He appeared in a career-high 68 games and collected 38 saves in 45 tries. Proving that he could be called on in the eighth inning when necessary, he recorded eight saves of four outs or more, tops in the majors.

Few people expected the Giants to be serious contenders in 2010, despite an outstanding starting rotation. But while the team scored runs at a rate below the league average, they continued to win games with pitching, and if they could take a lead into the ninth, Wilson usually locked it down. The colorful closer had his best season to date in 2010, with an ERA of 1.81 and major-league-leading 48 saves. Giants opponents came to dread his end-of-game ritual: after recording the final out, Wilson turns to face center field, looks skyward and crosses his arms to make an "X," with his right index finger extended. The gesture is packed with meaning: it's a nod to mixed-martial arts culture, a reflection of his Christianity and a sign that honors his father's memory.

On October 3, Wilson picked up his final save of the regular season as the Giants defeated the San Diego Padres to clinch the NL West. In the first postseason of his career, all of Wilson's fire and fury were unleashed on his opponents. He was victimized by an unearned run in his first appearance in Game 2 of the NLDS, but he was spotless after that. He saved Games 3 and 4 to close out Atlanta, and then slammed the door in Games 1 and 3 against the Phillies. He earned the win in Game 4 of that series and then clinched the pennant with a five-out save in Game 5, which ended when he caught Ryan Howard looking with two men on base.

Wilson's first two World Series appearances were not save situations, but in Game 5 he entered with the Giants leading both the series and the game 3–1, and with the heart of the Texas Rangers' batting order coming up. He froze Josh Hamilton on a called strike three to lead off the ninth, then induced Vlad Guerrero to hit a weak roller to third. That brought up Nelson Cruz, who worked the count full before Wilson blew him away with an inside fastball to clinch the championship. Overall, in 10 playoff matches, Wilson twirled 11 innings and surrendered just five hits without allowing an earned run. In all three series-clinching games, "X" marked the save.

$24.95
GATE 12
SECTION CLUB
SEAT S2
G7SS128
110CT11

CAREER HIGHLIGHTS

- led majors with a combined 127 saves from 2008 through 2010
- has converted 134 of 154 save opportunities (87 percent) over his career
- two-time NL All-Star (2008, 2010)

38 RELIEF PITCHER
Brian WILSON

AMERICAN LEAGUE

ELVIS ANDRUS - Texas Rangers

TREVOR CAHILL - Oakland Athletics

NEFTALI FELIZ - Texas Rangers

AUSTIN JACKSON - Detroit Tigers

RICKY ROMERO - Toronto Blue Jays

DANNY VALENCIA - Minnesota Twins

NATIONAL LEAGUE

STARLIN CASTRO - Chicago Cubs

JASON HEYWARD - Atlanta Braves

ANDREW McCUTCHEN - Pittsburgh Pirates

BUSTER POSEY - San Francisco Giants

GABY SANCHEZ - Florida Marlins

STEPHEN STRASBURG - Washington Nationals

Rough
DIAMONDS

ROUGH DIAMONDS

53 TREVOR CAHILL
PITCHER

1 ELVIS ANDRUS
SHORTSTOP

30 ROOKIE
NEFTALI FELIZ
PITCHER

Texas Rangers

- was second in AL Rookie of the Year voting in 2009 after ranking among the league's best defensive shortstops at age 20
- stole 33 bases as a rookie, then swiped 32 more in 2010
- appeared in the 2010 All-Star Game, then batted .294 with eight stolen bases in the 2010 postseason

1 ELVIS ANDRUS
SHORTSTOP

Oakland Athletics

- led MLB rookies with 32 starts and won 10 games in 2009 at 21 years old
- posted an 18–8 record and a 2.97 ERA in his sophomore season in 2010
- named to the 2010 AL All-Star Team

53 TREVOR CAHILL
PITCHER

Texas Rangers

- named AL Rookie of the Year and an All-Star in 2010 as he emerged as one of the game's top closers
- set MLB record for rookies with 40 saves (in 43 opportunities), then added another in the World Series
- throws a fastball that has been clocked at 101 miles per hour

30 ROOKIE
NEFTALI FELIZ
PITCHER

14 ROOKIE
AUSTIN JACKSON
OUTFIELD

24 RICKY ROMERO
PITCHER

19 ROOKIE
DANNY VALENCIA
THIRD BASE

Detroit Tigers

- led AL freshmen in runs, hits, total bases, extra-base hits, doubles, triples and stolen bases in 2010

- fourth player in modern MLB history to collect 100 runs, 180 hits, 30 doubles, 10 triples and 25 steals as a rookie

- chosen by *Sporting News* as the 2010 AL Rookie of the Year

14 ROOKIE
AUSTIN JACKSON
OUTFIELD

Toronto Blue Jays

- selected in the first round of the 2005 draft after leading Cal State Fullerton to a College World Series championship

- went 13–9 with 141 strikeouts as a rookie in 2009

- posted a 14–9 record in 2010 and led the Toronto staff with 210 innings pitched, including three complete games

24 RICKY ROMERO
PITCHER

Minnesota Twins

- made his MLB debut in 2010 as a late-blooming 25-year-old and batted .311 with a .448 slugging percentage

- became the first Twins player to hit a grand slam for his first major-league home run on July 26, 2010

- named to the *Baseball America* and Topps All-Rookie teams

19 ROOKIE
DANNY VALENCIA
THIRD BASE

ROUGH DIAMONDS

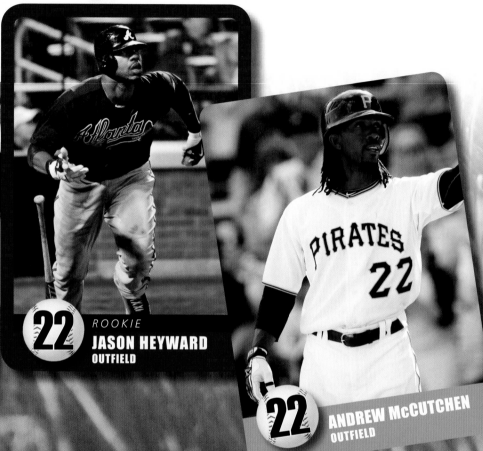

ROOKIE
STARLIN CASTRO
SHORTSTOP

13

22
ROOKIE
JASON HEYWARD
OUTFIELD

22
ANDREW McCUTCHEN
OUTFIELD

Chicago Cubs

- batted .300 with 31 doubles as a 20-year-old rookie in 2010
- set an MLB record with six RBIs in first major-league game, including a three-run homer in his first career at-bat and a bases-loaded triple
- had 39 multi-hit games, the most by a Cubs rookie since 1988

Atlanta Braves

- selected as *Baseball America's* and *USA Today's* Minor League Player of the Year in 2009, when he batted .323 with 17 homers in 99 games
- batted .277 with 18 homers, 72 RBIs, a .393 on-base percentage in his 2010 rookie campaign
- named to the 2010 All-Star Team and was runner-up for NL Rookie of the Year Award

Pittsburgh Pirates

- selected in the first round by the Pirates in the 2005 draft
- named *Baseball America's* 2009 Rookie of the Year after posting a .365 OBP and a .471 slugging percentage in 108 games
- led the 2010 Pirates in hits (163), doubles (35), walks (70) and stolen bases (33) during his first full season

13
ROOKIE
STARLIN CASTRO
SHORTSTOP

22
ROOKIE
JASON HEYWARD
OUTFIELD

22
ANDREW McCUTCHEN
OUTFIELD

28 ROOKIE
BUSTER POSEY
CATCHER

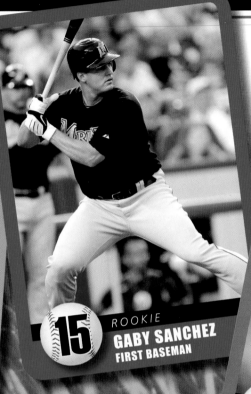

15 ROOKIE
GABY SANCHEZ
FIRST BASEMAN

37 ROOKIE
STEPHEN STRASBURG
PITCHER

San Francisco Giants

- drafted fifth overall in 2008 after winning the Golden Spikes Award (best amateur player) and Johnny Bench Award (best college catcher) that year
- voted 2010 NL Rookie of the Year after leading all freshmen with a .305 average and .505 slugging percentage
- first rookie catcher to bat cleanup in a World Series, during which he hit .300 in five games

28 ROOKIE
BUSTER POSEY
CATCHER

Florida Marlins

- drafted by the Seattle Mariners in 2005 and did not play a full season in the majors until age 26
- led all 2010 rookies with 37 doubles, 85 RBIs, 59 extra-base hits, and 256 total bases
- named to the *Baseball America* and Topps All-Rookie teams

15 ROOKIE
GABY SANCHEZ
FIRST BASEMAN

Washington Nationals

- drafted first overall by the Nationals in 2009 and considered one of the top pitching prospects of all-time
- made his major-league debut on June 8, 2010, and set an MLB record with 14 strikeouts in his first game
- posted a 5–3 record, a 2.91 ERA and 92 strikeouts in 68 innings in his injury-shortened first season

37 ROOKIE
STEPHEN STRASBURG
PITCHER

20–20 club: players who have collected 20 home runs and 20 stolen bases in the same season (also 30–30 club, 40–40 club)

AL: American League

ALCS: American League Championship Series

ALDS: American League Division Series

assist: a throw by a fielder that results in a putout

call-up: a minor-league player who is promoted to the major leagues in September, when the active roster expands from 25 to 40 players. Late-season call-ups are not eligible to play in the postseason

complete game: a game in which the starting pitcher is not removed for a relief pitcher

cycle: hitting a single, double, triple and home run in the same game

disabled list: a list of injured players who have been temporarily removed from the active roster in order to make room for a replacement. A player is placed on either the 15-day or 60-day disabled list and may not be activated until the end of that period

DL: disabled list

DP: double play

ERA: earned run average

fielding percentage: a statistical measure of a player's defensive ability, calculated by dividing assists and putouts by total chances